Railway Memories No

RETURN
TO
LEEDS

Robert Anderson & Peter Rose

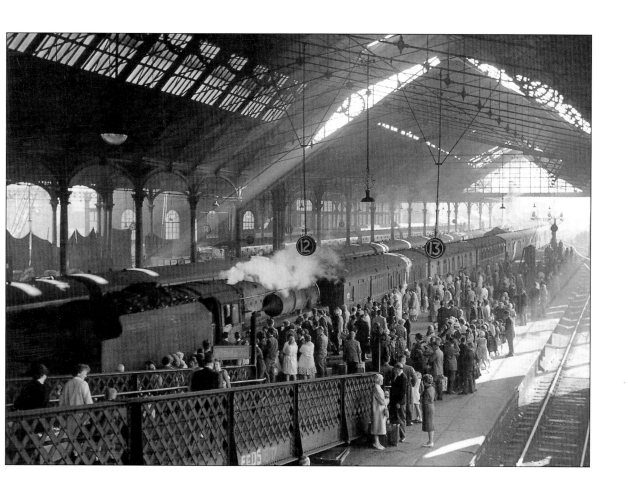

BELLCODE BOOKS
21 DALE AVENUE
TODMORDEN WEST YORKSHIRE OL14 6BA
email: bellcode4books@yahoo.co.uk

LNER D49 4-4-0 No. 2752 *The Atherstone* makes a splendid sight as she gets away from Leeds Central with an express towards Harrogate some time between 31st March 1946 and 12th April 1948. *Bob Lingwood/Peter Rose collection*

Copyright © 2009 Bellcode Books
ISBN 978-1-871233-22-3

Edited by Steve Chapman

Printed in the UK by the Amadeus Press, Ltd., Cleckheaton, West Yorkshire.

FRONT COVER: The Compound 4-4-0s are close to the end of their time and Lancaster-based No. 41101, almost certainly the last one to be seen active in Leeds, is in pretty deplorable condition as she leaves Leeds City North with a stopping train to Morecambe in May 1959. Appearances of 41101 were by this time very spasmodic and this would be one of her very last workings. *Colour-Rail BRM1956*
BACK COVER TOP: LNER K4 2-6-0 No. 3442 *The Great Marquess*, preserved by Viscount Garnock, waits to leave Cross Gates station with a special towards Leeds in March 1963. Since then, the station has been stripped of its platform buildings and canopies while the through fast lines have also been removed. *Jack Wild/Stephen Chapman archive*
BACK COVER BOTTOM: Holbeck celebrity motive power, 1990s style. BR/Sulzer Type 2(Class 25) No. D7672 *Tamworth Castle*(formerly 25912), restored at Holbeck depot in 1989 as a training exercise, departs Leeds City station with its last main line run, The Rat Requiem railtour to Holyhead, on 30th March 1991. *Stephen Chapman*
FRONTISPIECE: Filthy, decrepit and oozing atmosphere - the original Leeds City South on Saturday 12th August 1961. Excited daytrippers pack the platform as Standard Class 5 4-6-0 No. 73166 arrives from Neville Hill with empty stock for a holiday extra which it will run round and work to Scarborough. *Peter Rose*

Amendments to previous Railway Memories books: Railway Memories No.21: Page 55 bottom: this picture should be in this book - it is Holbeck shed! Page 71 top: More information on this picture - *Morthoe* is on the Swinton curve, from Mexborough to the Midland line; Page 94 bottom: David Muffitt advises that the EM1 is on its way up the bank to assist a train from West Silkstone Colliery. Page 100 bottom: This charming picture is Nunnery Colliery, Sheffield, not Hepworth Iron Co. The loco is one of two 0-6-0 tanks built for the North Staffordshire Railway but not required. Page 79 and 78 bottom: The date should read 12th September 1959.

Our thanks are due to all those who have so willingly provided material and assistance for this edition of Railway Memories including Robert Anderson, Ken Appleby, Leeds Local History Library, Tom Greaves and Ron Hollier. **Information for this book** about the 1950s and later has come mainly from original sources, especially British Railways documents, but for historical information we acknowledge the following: Regional History of Railways books, South & West Yorkshire by David Joy, and North East England by Ken Hoole(David & Charles;) Railway Memories No.3 Leeds(Bellcode Books;) BR Steam Shed Allocations by P.B. Hands; contemporary editions of Modern Railways, Railnews, Railway Magazine,The Railway Observer and Trains Illustrated.

Requests for photographs published in Railway Memories will be passed automatically to the copyright holder and under normal circumstances Bellcode Books itself will not reply to readers making such requests.

INTRODUCTION

Leeds may not readily be counted among the traditional great railway towns but from the very birth of railways, it has been one of the most important. In some ways the most important.

The world's first proper railway was opened there little more than half way through the 18th century and from 1812 its trains were hauled by the world's first commercially successful steam locomotive. It is often said that the combined locomotive manufacturers of Leeds built more railway engines than either Crewe, Derby, Doncaster or Swindon.

The new main line railways of the 19th century found the growing industrial and commercial wealth of Leeds irrestistable and four of them had their own lines into the city while two more enjoyed running powers. The result was a diversity of motive power and general railway interest still to be savoured in the 1950s and 1960s.

The Leeds railway scene is constantly evolving and it has changed dramatically since Railway Memories No.3 was published in 1992 - what other city can say its main railway terminus has been totally rebuilt twice since 1960. Consequently, coverage of what might be termed the "modern era" - from the 1970s up to completion of the rebuilding of Leeds station in 2002 - is included.

Apologies to those readers who already have Railway Memories No.3 for the inevitable repetition of a few items. At least the many of you who didn't manage to get hold of the first book will be able to enjoy a small glimpse of it.

Contents

On 7th September 1964 British Railways began using the 24-hour clock in its working timetables so we use am and pm up to that date and thereafter the 24-hour clock except where direct comparisons are made between times in different eras.

Some pictures in this book are credited to John Beaumont and others to John Beaumont/Robert Anderson archive. These are two different John Beaumonts.

It's easy to forget that the 1960s Leeds City station was built when steam was still very much alive. On 29th May 1964 Neville Hill A1 Pacific No. 60131 *Osprey* **awaits departure with the 11am Liverpool-Newcastle, diverted via Horsforth instead of the booked Wetherby route. The A1 was deputising for the regular diesel which had derailed at Liverpool.** *Robert Anderson*

SETTING THE SCENE

George Stephenson wasn't even born when the Middleton Railway, sanctioned by Act of Parliament in 1758, began carrying coal from Middleton Colliery to the banks of the River Aire, making Leeds the world's first railway town.

At first its coal tubs were pulled by horses but in 1812 - thirteen years before Stephenson's *Locomotion* made its debut on the Stockton & Darlington Railway - the *Salamanca*, built by Leeds engineer Matthew Murray and using Middleton Colliery manager John Blenkinsop's rack adhesion system, was working trains to Leeds.

Not only was it the world's first commercially successful steam locomotive, but it also started a distinguished locomotive building tradition in Leeds lasting more than 180 years.

The city acquired its first passenger main line as early as September 1834 when the Leeds & Selby Railway started running from its terminus in Marsh Lane.

Not long after, the so-called Railway King, George Hudson, got in on the act by making Leeds a key part of the developing national rail network. His North Midland Railway, opened in July 1840, ran to Derby from its own terminus at Hunslet Lane and through links with other companies gave Leeds its first direct route to London.

Next in town was the Manchester & Leeds(the Lancashire & Yorkshire from 1847) which crossed the Pennines via Hebden Bridge and Normanton, from where it enjoyed running powers over the North Midland line to Hunslet Lane.

Marsh Lane, on the other hand, lost its passenger trains when another Hudson enterprise, the York & North Midland Railway, took a lease on the financially-troubled Leeds & Selby in November 1840 and promptly routed all its services to Hunslet Lane via Castleford and Methley. Through goods traffic was similarly diverted in 1848, Hudson arguing that Marsh Lane was too isolated and did not connect with other railways.

A local passenger service was restored in 1850 but the overall situation remained until 1869 when Marsh Lane was finally linked to the rest of the Leeds system.

In 1846 a third terminus was established when the Leeds & Bradford Railway(from Bradford Forster Square) set up Wellington station on a site close to the present City station. Again, Hudson was quick to capitalise and the Midland Railway(formed when the North Midland amalgamated with the Midland Counties and Derby Junction railways) made a connection to Wellington, transferring its passenger operations from Hunslet Lane.

Next came the Huddersfield & Leeds, opened in 1848 and forming a second, more direct route across the Pennines.

Then, on 9th July 1849, the Leeds & Thirsk Railway(later part of the Leeds Northern Railway and from 1854 the North Eastern Railway) opened its line to the north through Headingley.

The Great Northern Railway reached Leeds in 1854 when its Leeds, Bradford & Halifax Junction line met the Huddersfield & Leeds(by this time part of the London & North Western Railway) at Holbeck Junction on the approach to Central station. Three years later, the GNR opened another line into the city,

this time from Wakefield and forming the second and, ultimately, fastest link with London, to King's Cross via Doncaster. The Manchester, Sheffield & Lincolnshire Railway(the Great Central from 1899) had running powers into Leeds over this line.

The next step was to close the gap between Marsh Lane and the rest of the system, which the NER did on 1st April 1869 when it opened the raised section from the old terminus to a grand new city centre station built jointly with the LNWR.

Situated immediately along the south side of Wellington station, this was simply called New station. On 2nd May 1938 the two were combined and renamed Leeds City, Wellington being known as City(North) and New as City(South.)

Concurrently with the extension from Marsh Lane, the NER opened its line from Micklefield to Church Fenton, providing a more direct route between Leeds and York.

In 1876, the Midland's newly-opened Carlisle line put Wellington station on a direct route to Scotland; from 1882 the so-called Viaduct line from Farnley Junction enabled the LNWR's trains to run directly into Leeds New without passing congested Whitehall Junction, while the last main line into Leeds was opened, also by the LNWR, in 1900. Appropriately called the New Line, it ran from Heaton Lodge Junction, just north of Huddersfield, to join the existing Huddersfield & Leeds route by a flying junction at Farnley.

Completing the jig-saw were lines opened by the GNR from Beeston Junction(on the Leeds-Wakefield line) in 1898 and the NER from Neville Hill in 1899 to serve their neighbouring goods depots at Hunslet East. The two were not directly linked to form a through route but were connected by exchange sidings between the depots.

Other lines in the area which brought traffic directly into Leeds were the NER line from Wetherby to Cross Gates, completed in 1876, the GN line from Tingley to Beeston Junction, opened in 1890, and the East & West Yorkshire Union Railway which when completed in 1903 came into Stourton from Ardsley via Rothwell.

Numerous private sidings, often with their own shunting locomotives, served a variety of industrial concerns such as the Monk Bridge Iron & Steel company's foundry next to Holbeck Low Level which had a green side tank and a red saddletank. Industrial lines also served collieries such the Waterloo Colliery system which connected to the main line network at Neville Hill, and at Hunslet East where it also provided a connection to the Knostrop sewage works. The Aberford Railway running north from Garforth was intended to move coal from the collieries of Leeds & Selby Railway director Richard Gascoigne to the Great North Road at Aberford but for a time it also carried passengers. Originally worked by horses and gravity, it later used Manning Wardle saddletanks. It closed in 1924 after many of the pits it served were worked out and new bus services took away its passengers. Parts of the route can still be traced in 2009.

With a great tradition in locomotive building, it is claimed that together the manufacturers in Leeds built more locomo-

The first main line into Leeds was the Leeds & Selby Railway which from 1840 connected with the Hull & Selby Railway to form a through route between Leeds and Hull. On 8th June 1960, K3 2-6-0 No. 61932 clatters a Hull-Liverpool express complete with fish van over Garforth Junction, just over seven miles east of Leeds, where the line to Kippax and Castleford diverged away right. The junction was abolished in 1969 when the Castleford line ceased to be a through route. *Peter Cookson/Neville Stead collection*

tives than Crewe, Derby, Doncaster or Swindon. The great names of Hunslet Engine Co., Hudswell, Clarke & Co., and Manning Wardle lined the legendary Jack Lane in Hunslet, with Kitson & Co.'s Airedale Foundry and John Fowler's Steam Plough and Locomotive Works nearby, and Greenwood & Batley's Albion Works in Armley Road.

Passenger services

Throughout the 20th century Leeds became a major crossroads for some of the country's most famous and romantic named expresses.

 Arguably, the most important of these were, as they are today, the trains between Leeds and London King's Cross which until 1967 ran from Central station. They included magnificent Pullman trains such as the Queen of Scots which ran between King's Cross and Glasgow via Harrogate. On Mondays to Fridays in summer 1957, the northbound train - leaving King's Cross at noon - reached Leeds Central at 3.28pm, departing for the north at 3.37 following reversal and engine change. The southbound train - 11am from Glasgow Queen Street - arrived at 4.34pm, departed at 4.45 and raced to London in 3 hours 27 minutes(a different page in the summer 1957 timetable shows it completing the run in 3 hours 25 minutes) to be the fastest train on the route at the time. The Yorkshire Pullman, which conveyed through Pullman cars from Bradford Exchange and Harrogate, left at 10.50am and reached London in 3 hours 55 minutes. The return train left King's Cross at 5.30pm to arrive

Central station in 3 hours 47 minutes at 9.17pm, the Harrogate portion leaving at 9.27. Seven other trains ran each way between Leeds and King's Cross. Among them were the morning businessmen's train The West Riding, introduced in 1937 as The West Riding Limited(one of the LNER's famous streamlined expresses.) In 1957 it left Central at 7.50am and reached London in 3 hours 58 minutes, the return from King's Cross pulling into Central at 7.32pm. There was also The White Rose which arrived from King's Cross at 12.43pm, the return departing at 3.25. The 11.17am to King's Cross was a through train from Ripon. In addition to these were a number of through carriage portions which combined with or detached from other East Coast main line services at Doncaster. These included the 2pm from Leeds, shown on some public timetable pages as through carriages but on others as a through train. Originating from Harrogate, it combined at Doncaster with a portion from Hull and Bridlington. The 6.26pm from Leeds combined at Doncaster with a Newcastle-King's Cross train, making it to London in 3 hours 47 minutes. Extra portions ran on Fridays. The 2.59pm arrival from London conveyed through carriages to Ripon and the 6.40pm arrival through carriages to Harrogate. The 7.50am King's Cross-Newcastle conveyed through carriages for Leeds which were due to arrive in 3 hours 38 minutes at 11.28.

There were, of course, variations to the service on Saturdays, especially in the summer, while none of the afore-mentioned named trains ran on Sundays. The one named train on a Sunday was The Harrogate Sunday Pullman which arrived in Leeds Central at 1.26pm, going forward to Harrogate at 1.34 with a

5

Until 1967 Leeds' most glamourous expresses, not least the Pullmans, ran from Central station pulled by locomotives of the highest calibre. With chime whistle blowing, A4 Pacific No. 60003 *Andrew K. McCosh* starts the White Rose out of Central on its run to King's Cross while the Pullman cars of the northbound Queen of Scots await their departure for Glasgow. *J.K. Morton/Neville Stead collection*

Central station opened in 1849 but the story of its early years is unbelievably complicated - even chaotic because of disagreements between its four partners, the Leeds & Thirsk, the L&Y, the LNWR, and the Great Northern.

portion for Bradford Exchange departing at 1.39. The London-bound train left Harrogate at 3.50pm, arrived in Central at 4.20 and, after combining the Bradford portion, left at 4.30 for the capital which it reached at 8.9pm.

The Midland Railway was the first to introduce Pullman cars to this country with a service from Bradford Forster Square to London but the Midland line had no such trains from Leeds in the "Railway Memories" era. It did, however, boast the famous St. Pancras-Glasgow Thames-Clyde Express, as well as a St. Pancras-Edinburgh express once named the Thames-Forth and, from June 1957 - after a spell of anonymity - The Waverley which was, curiously, not advertized as named in the summer 1957 timetable. On Mondays to Saturdays in summer 1957, the Thames-Clyde from Glasgow St. Enoch (dep 9.20am) was booked to pull into Leeds City North at 2.21pm and depart for St. Pancras at 2.27 - a very sharp turnround for a reversal and loco change. No sooner was that dealt with than the northbound train(10.15am from St. Pancras) arrived at 2.35pm, after a 4 hours 20 minutes 4-6-0-hauled run which compared well with the more usual 3 hours 50-odd minutes behind a Pacific on the East Coast route. It too was away after only six minutes, leaving for Carlisle and Glasgow at 2.41. Similarly slick work was required in turning round the 9.15am St. Pancras-Edinburgh - The Waverley - which was even faster from London, reaching Leeds City North in 4 hours 17 minutes at 1.32pm and departing for the north at 1.38. The 10.5am from Edinburgh arrived in Leeds at 3.18pm and was away again at 3.24 for its 4 hour 26 minute sprint to St. Pancras.

Six other trains left Leeds City for St.Pancras each weekday and four arrived from St. Pancras, most advertized as through trains to/from Bradford Forster Square. At night, sleeping car trains ran each way between St. Pancras and Glasgow, St. Pancras and Edinburgh and from St. Pancras to Leeds. Some additional trains ran on Fridays while times varied on Saturdays.

One other named train on the Midland was the Bradford Forster Square-Paignton "Devonian." In summer 1957 it left Leeds City at 10.20am on weekdays(9.43 on Saturdays,) the northbound train arriving from the West Country at 6.23pm (6.20 on Saturdays) before continuing to its journey's end at Bradford. Two more trains from Leeds City to Bristol and two from Birmingham to Leeds(to/from Bradford) made up the total weekday Cross-Country service at that time. Extra trains ran on summer Saturdays, especially to/from Bournemouth and Paignton while there were also a handful of weekday trains between Bradford, Leeds and Derby or Nottingham.

Making up a total of eight named expresses serving Leeds in

summer 1957 was The North Briton. Leaving Leeds City South at 9.15am, it ran via York and Newcastle to Glasgow Queen Street. The return service, 4pm from Glasgow, reached Leeds at 10.3pm. A relief train ran on Mondays, leaving Leeds City at 8.50am.

Also using Leeds City South were the Trans-Pennine expresses between Liverpool Lime Street and Hull or Newcastle. The Newcastle trains, which generally took the Leeds Northern route, originally reversed at Leeds to run via Headingley but a new spur completed at Wetherby in 1902 enabled them to avoid the Leeds reversal. In the 1940s and '50s the Wetherby line's steep gradients saw these trains gravitate back to the Headingley route. When diesels took over in 1961, firstly the English Electric Type 4s(Class 40s) and then the Class 46 "Peaks," they were able to resume the Wetherby road but only until its closure in 1964. With the closing of the Leeds Northern north of Harrogate in March 1967, all such trains had then to run via York. In summer 1957, three Liverpool-Newcastle trains each way on weekdays served Leeds City, plus three from Hull to Liverpool and two from Liverpool to Hull. Various extras included Leeds-Manchester Exchange trains with through carriages to Liverpool, Leeds-Stockport through carriages, a summer weekday 10am Sunderland-Manchester Exchange, a 4.10pm Sunderland to Liverpool Exchange on Fridays departing Leeds City at 6.48pm, the 9.50pm York-Liverpool mail and 10.40pm return with through carriages to/from Swansea, additional Manchester Exchange-Newcastle

trains on Mondays and Fridays, and through carriages via Manchester Exchange from Wigan North Western and Blackpool Central to Leeds.

Another Trans-Pennine service reaching Leeds - Central station in this case - was the service from Liverpool Exchange via the L&Y. In steam days Leeds portions were attached and detached to/from Bradford trains at Low Moor or Halifax, but when the specially-designed Calder Valley Class 110 diesel multiple units took over in 1962 all trains were routed via Bradford Exchange and most extended to/from Harrogate.

A whole myriad of other services ran in and out of Leeds. From Central station in the 1950s, they went to Doncaster, Cleethorpes, Castleford Central via Stanley, Bradford Exchange via Stanningley or Pudsey Lowtown and Greenside, Huddersfield via Halifax, Blackpool Central, and to Knaresborough and Ripon via Headingley. Services once ran between Central, Batley, Dewsbury, Barnsley, Wakefield and Bradford Exchange via Beeston and Tingley but by 1950 only four weekday trains from Leeds to Wakefield plus five return, and a summer Saturday Leeds-Tingley-Bradford train, remained, these services being withdrawn on 29th October 1951.

From City station they ran to York, Scarborough, Whitby and Hull, to Bridlington via Selby and Market Weighton, Huddersfield, Blackpool, Penistone and Stockport, Goole via Castleford Cutsyke, Ilkley via Otley, Skipton via Shipley and via Guiseley and Ilkley, Sheffield Midland via Cudworth, Bradford Forster Square, Morecambe and Lancaster, West

The nine A3 Pacifics transferred to Holbeck shed in 1960 for Settle & Carlisle work proved popular with the Holbeck enginemen. One of them, No. 60038 *Firdaussi*, gets into its stride at Whitehall Junction with the northbound Thames-Clyde Express, 2.44pm from Leeds, on 15th August 1961. Unlike her classmates which were all transferred away by July 1961, *Firdaussi* stayed at Holbeck until June 1963 when she moved to Neville Hill. *Peter Rose*

Hartlepool, Middlesbrough, Northallerton and Thirsk via Harrogate, and Tadcaster via Wetherby. Until January 1951 a push-pull service operated by ex-NER G5 0-4-4Ts ran via Garforth and Kippax to Castleford Central where they met head-on with the trains from Central.

Among Leeds' many railway firsts were the first of the diesel multiple units that were by the 1960s to flood the country's rail network. These Derby Works-built pioneers began operation on Leeds Central-Bradford Exchange and other services in 1954. Despite teething problems requiring steam substitutions, they were a huge success, attracting 80,000 more Leeds-Bradford passengers between mid-June and the end of September with similar growth on the other routes. More came from the late 1950s to take over most local services, rendering many older steam passenger locos redundant. In January 1961 DMU transformed the Trans-Pennine service when six-car Inter-City sets purpose-built in Swindon began their 20-year association with the route. They included a revolutionary catering concept - the Griddle - which, well ahead of its time, served Aberdeen Angus burgers, and bangers & mash. The service was increased to five trains each way with extras between Leeds and Liverpool. An hourly Leeds-Huddersfield local DMU service was introduced at the same time. The Trans-Pennines were an instant hit, increasing the number of Leeds-Liverpool passenger journeys by a staggering 45 per cent in their first week. Together with Type 4 locomotives on the Newcastle-Liverpools they eradicated steam from the route but for the Friday 5.37pm Manchester-Newcastle and a couple of Sunday trains

- although the new diesels broke down with tedious regularity and steam was often called to the rescue right up to early 1968.

As the 1960s passed into the 1970s, the famous expresses serving Leeds lost their names or disappeared amidst the many evolutionary timetable changes necessary to meet changing demand and travel patterns, the emphasis now on business travel. The age of romanticism had given way to corporatism, standardization of service and the BR all-blue regime.

The 1973/74 timetable advertized the Yorkshire Pullman as the only Leeds(start Harrogate 09.52)-King's Cross named train, but the Deltic-hauled 07.30 from Leeds, which ran non-stop and did the journey in 2hrs 32 minutes was now the peak business train to London, fulfilling the role of the old West Riding and set to become the Leeds Executive. The Pullman provided the return fast business service, leaving King's Cross at 17.05 and reaching Leeds City in just 2 hrs 24 minutes before continuing to Harrogate. The Thames-Clyde, The North Briton and The Devonian were at this time still named, while the 07.41 Leeds-Penzance and 10.25 return had become The Cornishman. By 1978 all these time-honoured names had been dropped or were no longer advertized. The Yorkshire Pullman survived until Friday 5th May when, Deltic-hauled, it made its last run. The following Monday the new East Coast main line InterCity 125 timetable came into force and the Pullman's place was taken by the Leeds Executive which became a 125 and, stated BR publicity, provided Pullman-style service without the supplementary charge.

During the early 1980s Leeds regained another named train

A classic GN lines local passenger train during the transition to diesel multiple units. Having departed Leeds Central, Copley Hill N1 0-6-2T No. 69440 approaches Holbeck High Level station in October 1954. *Neville Stead collection*

The first full fleet operation of diesel multiple units in the country. Complete with oil tail lamp, a Derby Works lightweight set, car No. E79500 nearest the camera, leaves Leeds Central for Bradford Exchange on 27th August 1954. *H. Walshaw/Photos from the Fifties*

when it was also served by the Bradford Executive, forced to run via Leeds following the controversial closure of the Wortley curve which had provided a direct route between the Bradford Exchange and the Doncaster line. A third named train of the time was The West Yorkshire Executive - a business train from London fulfiling the role of the old White Rose but it lasted only two years, from May 1984 to May 1986. Executive was an over-used 1970s word - executive cars, executive homes and executive trains - totally lacking the charm and appeal of the old names. BR's newly-formed InterCity business must have thought so too because in May 1985 the Leeds Executive reverted to being the Yorkshire Pullman, but the Bradford Executive name was dropped a year later to leave the Yorkshire Pullman again the only named train. The White Rose made a comeback in 2001, being the generic name given to short-lived extra King's Cross trains run by Great North Eastern Railway - the new private operator of East Coast services - using hired Eurostar trains. They ran from York but were switched to Leeds following completion of the station reconstruction, although the name was no longer advertized in the timetable.They have since been replaced by regular half-hourly Leeds-King's Cross trains using conventional HSTs and InterCity 225 sets. No Leeds trains carry names in 2009.

On the Midland line, completion of the West Coast main line electrification in 1974 brought the end of through St. Pancras-Glasgow services which were replaced by just three Nottingham-Carlisle/Glasgow trains each way. These were rerouted via the West Coast and Manchester in the early 1980s to leave a Leeds-Carlisle service of just two trains each way as the Settle & Carlisle line was prepared for closure(which thankfully did not happen.) A Leeds-Nottingham service of five trains each way was introduced in May 1986 while the Leeds-

St. Pancras service, miraculously perhaps, just managed to hang on with the odd one or two trains each way. In 2009 the service is slightly better with two (very) early morning trains to St. Pancras and three evening returns although their main purpose is to return HST sets to Neville Hill depot for overnight maintenance.

The South West service from Leeds has increased considerably since the paucity of the 1960s, starting in the 1980s when some North East-South West expresses running direct between York and Sheffield were rerouted via Leeds. In 2009 Scotland-North East-South West and South Coast trains serve Leeds every hour during the day.

Trans-Pennine services were radically re-shaped in May 1979 when the time-honoured Hull-Liverpool through service was replaced by York-Liverpool trains hauled by Class 45, 46 or 47 locomotives, though the 40s still put in appearances up to 1983. The Trans-Pennine DMU sets, augmented by former Western Region Class 123 InterCity units, were relegated to working a Hull-Leeds shuttle and a few trains which still ran between Hull or York and Manchester plus some Morecambe trains. The Newcastle-Liverpool trains were upgraded with Brush Class 47 locos and, initially, air-conditioned coaches displaced from the ECML by HSTs. A memorable chapter for enthusiasts began in June 1979 when Deltics, also displaced from prime East Coast duties, began appearing on York-Liverpool trains which they continued to do until their final withdrawal at the end of 1981. Since then, the route has flourished in terms of service frequency, especially since new diesel units replaced loco-hauled trains in the late 1980s and early 1990s. The service has increased to four trains an hour between Leeds and Manchester, including hourly Hull-Manchester trains as well as hourly Newcastle-Manchester, Middlesbrough-

In the early 1980s Midland line trains between Leeds and the North were reduced to just two Leeds-Carlisle trains each way per day. In September 1985, Carlisle Kingmoor-based English Electric Type 4 No. D200(Class 40 No. 40122) awaits departure from Leeds City with the 15.55 to Carlisle. *Stephen Chapman*

Manchester and Scarborough-Liverpool services, operated in 2009 by Class 170(Hull) and Class 185 diesel units.

As with most places, many extra trains were run from Leeds on summer Saturdays to cater for the hordes of holidaymakers who traditionally began and finished their holidays on those few days of the year. Spare coaches were stored at various locations during the winter purely to meet summer Saturday demand which was such that even goods engines were pressed into passenger service. The most popular destinations from Leeds were Scarborough, Bridlington, Filey Holiday Camp where Butlin's had their own station, Whitby, Skegness, Blackpool and Morecambe while extra trains also ran to such far-off resorts as Bournemouth, Torquay and Paignton.

During the 1960s increasing car ownership, overseas package holidays, a severe pruning of the coaching stock fleet and, latterly, faster and more frequent regular services heralded a steady decline in summer Saturday extras until they had all but disappeared by the 1990s. A Skegness train(normally worked by a Brush Type 2) which ran from the late 1980s until 1991 was one of the last true loco-hauled summer Saturday services from Leeds. Then, in 2004, with its new Voyager multiple units (which had replaced loco-hauled trains and HSTs) proving woefully inadequate for summer holiday passengers and their luggage, the then Cross-Country operator Virgin was forced to run a loco-hauled summer Saturday return Newcastle-Leeds-Paignton relief using a Class 67 locomotive hired from freight operator EWS.

Freight traffic

Leeds was, and still is, an important centre for goods traffic,

once possessing no less than nine freight depots, four main sorting yards and numerous private sidings serving all manner of industries. Each of the old railway companies with lines into Leeds had their own sorting yards. The Midland had Stourton and Hunslet, the LNWR had the yard at Copley Hill and the North Eastern had sidings at Neville Hill. The GN had its big centre at Ardsley half way between Leeds and Wakefield.

According to the winter 1959/60 Working Timetable, Stourton handled a total of just over 70 booked incoming and outgoing trains every 24 hours on Mondays to Fridays with Hunslet Up and Down Sidings between them handling 57 arrivals and departures. Hunslet dealt with a whole variety of trains to and from such places as Carlisle, Heysham, Carnforth, Bradford, Goole, Sheffield, Heaton Mersey, Toton, Nottingham and Water Orton, but in the early morning the Down yard saw a succession of express freights, including Class C fully-braked trains from Birmingham Lawley Street, Bristol(continuing to Hunslet Lane,) Leicester, Somers Town, Nottingham and St. Pancras. Stourton also handled a range of trains to and from such places as Carnforth, Carlisle, Lancaster, Bradford, Heysham, Crofton, Rotherham, Derby, Normanton and Washwood Heath. The Down yard handled mainly mineral traffic and many were loose coupled class H or J trains, but in the late evening the Up yard dispatched class C or D expresses to St. Pancras, Leicester, Lawley Street, Washwood Heath and Nottingham(the latter pair originating at Bradford.) Local trips also ran between Stourton or Hunslet and Neville Hill, Copley Hill, Hunslet Lane, Guiseley, Apperley Bridge, Apperley Viaduct(for the Esholt sewage works siding,) Methley Sidings, Ilkley and Keighley.

Some fast long-distance freights passed through Leeds on the

Leeds freight in abundance. WD 2-8-0 No. 90503 of Thornaby shed, doubtless on a fill-in turn after bringing a freight from Teesside, passes Holbeck Low Level station and Geldard Junction signal box while returning the Otley pick-up to Neville Hill on 20th March 1961. On the left, a Stourton 4F 0-6-0 has left tanks in the gas works sidings and is collecting empty mineral wagons and loaded coke wagons.
Peter Rose

Midland without stopping, or only to stop for water or crew change. The two most important trains on the line were 3S60(accelerated class C No. 5022 in 1960) and 3M29(accelerated class C No. 5035,) the 7.23pm Hendon to Glasgow Gushetfaulds and 7.50pm Gushetfaulds to Hendon "Condor," booked to pass Stourton Junction at 11.59pm northbound and 42 minutes past midnight southbound. Initially powered by pairs of the ill-starred Metrovick Co-Bo diesels, this all-container service introduced in 1959 was a pioneer of the intermodal freight operation that is today so strongly represented in Leeds. The Condor ran until October 1967 when it was replaced by a Freightliner service. Other non-stop express freights included Water Orton-Carlisle class C and D freights, worked throughout by Saltley men and engines - usually 9F 2-10-0s, as well as Willesden-Carlisle, Leicester-Carlisle and Rotherham Masborough-Glasgow class Cs.

Copley Hill dealt with around 25 trains every 24 hours Monday to Friday to and from Huddersfield, Manchester Brewery Sidings, Patricroft, Mold Junction, Aintree, Birkenhead, Macclesfield, Widnes, Mirfield, Crewe, Lostock Hall and Stockport Adswood. A class C fully fitted express freight was booked to leave for Pontypool Road at 9.5pm, and at 9.45pm a class D to Aston and Manchester London Road, while a class C was booked to arrive from Grange Junction at 6.15am. In addition to these, there were no less than seven paths between 2pm and 10.20pm for class C arrivals from Garston Dock which ran when required.

Neville Hill saw around 30 arrivals and departures each 24 hours to and from Hull, York, Newport(Tees,) Darlington,

Stockton and Starbeck. They included a 6.10am pick-up to Otley, a return trip to Cardigan Road coal depot and trips to/ from Stourton and Hunslet.

In the early 1960s BR's North Eastern Region began replacing its many local sorting yards with big, central hump marshalling yards, of which Stourton was to be one. But the wagonload traffic they were meant to handle was declining and with another big yard nearby at Healey Mills, work at Stourton was halted and the yard closed along with all yards in Leeds, except Hunslet, when Healey Mills came into operation in 1964. The Freightliner terminal was built on the Stourton site.

The biggest goods depots in Leeds were the Midland's Hunslet Lane, which survived until the early 1980s, and the vast Wellington Street complex which included LNW and L&Y joint, GN and NE depots and stayed in business, much reduced, until 1974. Both the GN and NER had goods depots at Hunslet East, served by branches from Beeston and Neville Hill respectively. They closed in September 1966 and the site used for an oil terminal served only from the Neville Hill end. Hunslet East survives in 2009 but now deals with cement and aggregate trains.

Motive power depots

To service this mass of railway, Leeds once had no less than six functioning locomotive depots, each with its own distinct role and company lineage.

Top shed was Holbeck, opened by the Midland Railway in the late 1860s and supplier of prime passenger power for the old

11

Hunslet yards remained in operation for local traffic following completion of the big marshalling yard at Healey Mills in 1964. English Electric Type 4 No. 40009 barely gives them a second glance as it passes with the 6E54 Ribblehead-Healey Mills ballast train on 12th February 1980. The recently remodelled Down yard is on the left and the Up yard - the site in 2009 occupied by Midland Road locomotive and wagon depot - is on the right. *Peter Rose*

company's main lines. Over the years it became synonymous with the Compound 4-4-0s, Jubilee and Royal Scot 4-6-0s and, oddly, the ex-LNER A3 Pacifics drafted in for Carlisle expresses. Following dieselisation, it was home to the "Peaks" which so dominated Midland line services.

The last steam shed in Leeds, Holbeck closed to steam on 30th September 1967 after which most steam locomotives visiting the city had to be serviced at Normanton, 14 miles away. The last steam engine to leave Holbeck under its own power was Stanier Class 5 4-6-0 No. 45428, bound for preservation in Birmingham, on 24th August 1968. After some years as a diesel maintenance depot and then a diesel fuelling and stabling point, Holbeck became an engineers' plant depot, the role it still fulfils in 2009.

Stourton, situated alongside the Down sorting yard, supplied goods engines for the Midland and was accompanied by wagon workshops on the Up side of the main line. It closed altogether in January 1967 but the wagon shops survived intact until the 1980s when they were last used for storing surplus locomotives, wagons and officers' inspection saloons.

At Farnley Junction was the LNWR's shed providing goods and passenger power for the Trans-Pennine route. It closed completely in November 1966 when most of its allocation, including its Jubilees, went to Holbeck.

The NER shed was the large complex at Neville Hill, opened in 1904 to replace the old Leeds & Thirsk Railway roundhouses in Wellington Road. Its fleet was essentially North Eastern with Q6 0-8-0s, J21 and J39 0-6-0s, various 0-6-0Ts and G5 0-4-4Ts. For main line passenger work there were B1 and B16 4-6-0s, and D20 and D49 4-4-0s, but pride of the shed were its A3 and, latterly, A1 Pacifics.

After the opening of facilities for dealing with diesel multiple units and locomotives in May 1960, the first main line diesel locomotives in Leeds were allocated to Neville Hill, and consisted of two dozen English Electric Type 4s and BR/Sulzer "Peak" Type 4s.

Neville Hill became an all-diesel depot in June 1966 when its last steam locos - Q6 0-8-0s Nos. 63344, 63420 and 63426 were transferred to Normanton, and Fairburn 2-6-4Ts 42184 and 42196 to Low Moor and 42699 to Holbeck.

A three-year modernisation programme completed in 1978 included converting the roundhouse into a maintenance shed for High Speed Trains plus construction of cleaning and servicing sheds for coaches, DMUs and HSTs, establishing Neville Hill as one of Britain's principal depots for local and Inter-City trains.

Arguably the most glamourous shed in terms of engines dealt with was Copley Hill, the former GNR depot which was home to the LNER Pacifics working expresses to King's Cross. Not surprisingly, it succumbed early to diesels and closed completely in September 1964. The straight shed and its environs were demolished the following year.

These were not the only, nor the first locomotive depots in Leeds, though. The North Midland had an eight-road engine house at Hunslet Lane. It remained in use, probably for goods engines, until the 1870s when it was converted into a goods warehouse. There was also a Midland single turntable roundhouse on the south flank of Wellington station. It was replaced by Holbeck and demolished in 1869 to make room for the New station.

The Leeds & Thirsk depot in Wellington Road(also known as Holbeck) consisted of one full roundhouse and a half round house plus workshops. The NER updated the depot and added

A sight that inspired countless young enthusiasts in the 1950s - a big motive power depot packed with lines of simmering engines - and there were five of them in Leeds.

This view of Holbeck No.2 side taken from the coaling plant on 17th April 1952 shows, from left: 8F 2-8-0 48145, "Crab" 2-6-0 42797, Black Five 4-6-0 45186, 8Fs 48261 and 48070, Black Fives 45238 and 44984, 8Fs 48537 and 48159, Black Fives 44853 and 44664, 8F 48399 and Ivatt Class 4MT 2-6-0 No. 43116.

Peter Rose

an extra roundhouse in 1873 but, being inconveniently situated after the opening of New station and the lines from York and Wetherby, the NER moved to Neville Hill in 1904. The historic buildings survived and remain in non-rail use in 2009.

The one other main line company with a depot in Leeds was the Lancashire & Yorkshire which had a six-road shed alongside the GN's at Copley Hill. Amalgamation with the LNWR in 1922 and other companies including the Midland to form the London Midland & Scottish Railway in 1923 ultimately rendered the depot redundant and it closed in the 1930s.

All change

Throughout their history, the railways of Leeds have been constantly evolving. In fact, it is hard to think of anywhere else where the railway scene has been in such a state of perpetual change. Major changes have included the construction of the New station and the line to Marsh Lane in the 1860s, the Viaduct Line in 1882 - designed to ease growing congestion around Whitehall Junction and the western approaches to City (then 'New' station,) - the 1930s combination of Wellington and New stations to form Leeds City station complete with a new Art Deco concourse and hotel, the 1960s reshaping of the Leeds network beyond recognition which concentrated all trains on City station, and the equally radical changes made at the end of the 20th century.

In truth, the 1960s combination amounted to closing Central, converting City North into a parcels concentration depot, and rebuilding City South as a super-modern station handling all the

city's remaining passenger trains. Signalling in the immediate area was modernized and brought under the control of one power signal box in offices towering over the new City station, while the maze of lines at the west end was remodelled so that trains previously using Central could run into City station - or just plain Leeds as it was to become, and the bay platforms 9/10(west end) and 14/15(east end) converted to through platforms, the station master's office between them being demolished.

Work began in 1960 and, being undertaken in gradual stages, was not completed until 1st May 1967, the day when all remaining services were switched to City. The original scheme involved laying a new spur from Holbeck Junction to Whitehall Junction so that Bradford Exchange and Doncaster trains could reach City station. A flyover from Copley Hill to Whitehall Junction would enable King's Cross trains to by-pass Holbeck Junction, while the number of approach lines at the west end of City station would be increased from four to six. The lines from Holbeck Junction to Central would be abandoned, though using Central station as the parcels depot so that Leeds City North could be replaced by a car park was considered.

While all this was in progress, the Beeching Report was published. Several services running into Leeds were to be withdrawn and it became evident that with fewer trains, a more modest layout would suffice. The original plans to increase the west end approach line to six were dropped, as was the flyover, reducing the overall cost from £4.5 million to £2.75 million. Instead, the original LNW Huddersfield lines were realigned to join the Doncaster and Bradford lines at Holbeck junctions, all trains being funnelled into the new Holbeck-

Whitehall spur. In place of the flyover, the Viaduct line was abandoned between Farnley Junction and the intersection with the Doncaster line where it made a new Doncaster-facing junction, enabling King's Cross trains to avoid Holbeck and Whitehall junctions by using this former LNW route. Against a backdrop of severe service cuts and declining passenger numbers this would seem like the right thing to do at the time but it would bring serious difficulties 20 years later as fortunes turned back in favour of the railways.

The Beeching Axe fell heavily on West Yorkshire's passenger network. Leeds services withdrawn were those over the Cross Gates-Wetherby line from 6th January 1964; the Pudsey Loop on 15th June 1964; to Castleford via Stanley on 2nd November 1964; to Bradford Forster Square and Ilkley via Otley on 22nd March 1965. Even the LNWR's New Line was axed in 1965 when all Trans-Pennine services were rerouted via Dewsbury, the last train to use it being the 15.00 Liverpool to Newcastle which was retained from the end of the 1964 summer timetable until the statutory closure procedure was completed.

Decline set in during the late 1960s thanks to these closures and increasing road competition. Principal routes into Leeds were reduced from four to two tracks. Patronage of West Yorkshire services, most of which ran into Leeds by then, slumped to a mere six million passenger journeys a year. Threatened

services were kept going a year at a time by Government grant aid, awarded under the terms of the Transport Act 1968. The Leeds-Bradford Exchange, Leeds-Goole, Leeds-York, Leeds-Doncaster, Leeds-Harrogate, Leeds-Huddersfield, Leeds-Skipton-Morecambe, Leeds-Barnsley-Sheffield, Leeds-Rotherham-Sheffield, Leeds-Liverpool and Leeds-Hull services all received annual subsidies. Valiant efforts by British Rail in 1973 to market local services turned a 5 per cent annual decline in passengers into a 5 per cent increase in the six months to October, but it was in 1976, when the West Yorkshire Passenger Transport Executive began financially supporting the network that a remarkable turnround began.

Not only did the PTE's support ensure the retention of most remaining services, but over three decades since then an attractive range of fares and tickets, investment in new stations, improved services, electrification to Skipton, Ilkley and of the reinstated Bradford Forster Square service - even line reopenings, have seen the annual number of passenger journeys in West Yorkshire soar to the present 25 million.

By the mid-1980s it was apparent that the 1960s layout and station would be incapable of accommodating such growth while at the same time the 20 year-old infrastructure was life-expired and becoming increasingly unreliable.

The 1960s Leeds City station was dark and depressing, and

Demolition of the Victorian Leeds City South station was under way and construction of the City House office block well advanced on 15th June 1963 when Jubilee 4-6-0 No. 45654 *Hood* was taking charge of the summer service 10am Sunderland to Manchester Exchange at 12.35pm. *Robert Anderson*

Transition at Leeds City in 1967. Beneath the low, unspectacular roof of the new station, BR/Sulzer Type 2(Class 24) No. D5100 and Fairburn 2-6-4T No. 42066 arrive with the 11.55 Bradford Exchange to King's Cross at 12.21 on 9th June. The scene makes an interesting comparison with that on page 1. *Robert Anderson*

its box-like structure formed a wind tunnel which made waiting on its platforms a cold and draughty experience. Passenger facilities were spartan and the only refuge from the cold draught were some cramped and narrow shelters. The only platform-side catering amenities were a small kiosk in the opening between platforms 9 and 12, on the extreme south side of the station, and a counter on platform 5 at the rear of the main buffet whose main entrance was outside the ticket barriers on the concourse.

By the mid-1980s, operation of the station had become a nightmare for railway staff and passengers alike. Points and signal failures at Leeds were legendary, and by delaying long-distance trains they had a knock-on effect as far across the network as London, Newcastle, Manchester, Birmingham and Bristol. Despite this, passengers flocked back to the trains in droves and with more trains on practically all routes, the 1960s infrastructure reached crisis point. Further track rationalisation during the mid-1980s, including closure of the Viaduct line and singling of the freight line between Whitehall and Engine Shed junctions in 1987 did little to help.

In the late 1980s, electrification of the East Coast main line, including the line from Doncaster to Leeds, brought an opportunity to renew and update the layout but it was largely by-passed. Not only that, but the BR management structure then in force ensured that Leeds City was only partially electrified; the electrification was an InterCity business sector project and so only the lines used by its trains from King's Cross were

electrified. The opportunity to renew signalling was also spurned; it was immunized against interference from the high voltage but that was about as far as it went. This may have appeared a mistake at the time but any work then would have inhibited prospects for complete reconstruction and expansion of the layout, plans for which were already being prepared, while to wait for these to be implemented would have delayed the electrification - by 10 years as it turned out. It was nevertheless cause for celebration when the first passenger-carrying electric InterCity train - the 06.50 from King's Cross - arrived, unannounced, on Saturday 11th March 1989 with 91008 hauling an HST set specially adapted for push-pull operation. The rest of the station was ultimately electrified, mainly during the Leeds North West project which saw electrification of the lines to Skipton, Ilkley and Bradford Forster Square completed in September 1995. In conjunction with the electrification, Leeds City signal box took over control of the whole Leeds North West network as far west as its interface with Hellifield.

Meanwhile, the constrained and worn-out layout continued to cause problems, especially as by the mid-1990s the station was handling 829 trains and 50,000 passengers a day. Trains entering the station from the west were routinely delayed because of congestion at Leeds City West, Whitehall and Holbeck junctions - echoes of the late 19th century when the LNWR's solution was to by-pass the whole lot with the Viaduct line. Over a century later a solution to the same problem was being proposed. British Rail had already drawn up plans to increase the number of approach lines between Whitehall Junction and Leeds City West from four to six(as per the original 1960s scheme,) to reinstate the LNWR approach lines from Copley Hill to Whitehall Junction, enabling Trans-Pennine trains to by-pass Holbeck Junction, and to increase the number of station platforms. Reopening the Viaduct line was ruled out. The scheme was originally costed at £20 million but as it waited and waited for authorisation, inflation and add-ons doubled the price tag. When finally implemented at the turn of the century by BR's privatized successor, Railtrack, it had reached a staggering £245 million. But whereas the BR plans were for renewal and expansion of track and signalling only, the final project involved the entire rebuilding of the whole station into a national showpiece.

In the meantime, BR's station management made some modest but highly effective improvements to passenger facilities. A garden area with seats was created opposite the ticket barrier along the ends of bay platforms 2 and 3. But, far and away the most dramatic improvement was an enclosed glass waiting lounge and buffet replacing the kiosk between platforms 9 and 12, and still in use at the new station.

Transfer of remaining mail traffic to a purpose-built terminal at Doncaster in 1997 allowed an immediate increase in station capacity by returning the North side to passenger use. The concourse, closed to passengers and used as a car park since 1967, was restored to its Art-Deco magnificence and reopened with a variety of retail and catering outlets. The remaining platform was reopened for passenger trains and electrified for use by King's Cross services. With the remodelling pending, there was no platform renumbering and it became "Platform W" - W for Wellington, the North side's original name.

These changes were taking place during the privatisation of BR and with Leeds declared one of the 13 busiest stations in the country, general management and control of train movements came directly under Railtrack, BR's businesses still running the trains until they too were privatized. For a time, there were two station managers, one BR and one Railtrack.

The major rebuilding finally began in March 1999 under the "Leeds 1st." banner and took three years to complete. Leeds 1st included two extra bay platforms on the North side(besides platform W) and a new through platform and bay on the south side, increasing the number of platforms from 12(pre-W) to 17. The 1960s station - once likened to a silage barn - was completely swept away and replaced by a magnificent new train shed with a barrel-vaulted northlight roof whose brave design owed more to Victorian elegance and grandeur than modern utility. The cramped subway was replaced by a wide mall-like bridge with waiting, information and catering facilities from which trains can be seen coming and going as far away as Copley Hill. The freight-only Whitehall-Engine Shed Junction line was restored to double track to accommodate the increasing freight traffic travelling via the Leeds-Carlisle route. Track and signalling was totally renewed and, in testimony to remarkable 21st Century technology, brought under the control of York signalling centre.

Leeds 1st was fully completed in 2002 and already the new layout is becoming fully occupied with further increases to local services, half-hourly King's Cross trains and up to four Sheffield trains an hour. Possibilities for further expansion must now be limited but future plans include one or more new platforms on an abandoned part of the North station, currently a car park, while Leeds 1st included the Whitehall flyover as an optional extra which was not taken up.

The passenger station isn't the only side of Leeds to have undergone an astonishing revival. Despite the proximity of the Wakefield Europort freight terminal opened at Normanton in 1996, the Freightliner terminal at Stourton has gone from strength to strength. This, combined with the burgeoning coal traffic operated through the area by Freightliner Heavy Haul, has led to the establishment of a new locomotive and wagon maintenance depot at Midland Road, on a site once occupied by Hunslet Up yard. Since then, Hunslet Down Sidings, disused since the early 1990s, have been brought back into use for stabling Freightliner coal hopper wagons. On the east side of Leeds, the oil terminals at Hunslet East ceased to be rail served around the end of the 20th century but new aggregate and cement terminals have taken their place, as well as that of a stone terminal at Marsh Lane goods yard where, by August 2009, the sidings were again being used for stone traffic.

In 2009 Leeds sees more passengers and more trains than ever before with services, on long-distance routes especially, reaching an intensity unimaginable in the 1950s. Freight, although still a shadow of what it was - as is the case across the entire railway system - has made an amazing comeback in the Leeds area since the 1990s. Most remarkable of all, is the establishment of a new locomotive depot, keeping two depots active in the city that boasted no less than six in the 1920s. And, after over 250 years, the Middleton Railway steams on.

Signalling along the Midland Main Line from Calverley & Rodley to Methley *was shown by the The LMS Midland Division Sectional Appendix issued in March 1937 as Absolute Block on main/passenger lines and Train Signalling by Telegraph Bells on Goods lines.*

Signal boxes(with distances from previous boxes) were at: Newlay & Horsforth(1 mile 308yds from Calverley & Rodley,) Kirkstall Jn.(1 mile 990yds.,) Armley Canal Jn.(1122yds.,) Armley Station Jn.(1452yds.,) Wortley Jn.(858yds.,) Holbeck(308yds. - not a block post,) Whitehall Jn.(286yds.,) Engine Shed Jn.(660yds.,) Hunslet Goods Jn.(1452yds.,) Hunslet Station Jn.(814yds.,) Hunslet South Jn.(968yds.,) Wakefield Road(462yds.,) Stourton Down Sidings(366yds.,) Stourton Up Sidings(435yds.,) Stourton Jn.(220yds.,) Rothwell Haigh(1166yds.,) Waterloo Colliery Sidings(1 mile 594yds.,) Woodlesford(1188yds.,) Methley Sidings(1 mile 616yds.)

Additional running lines were: Up & Down Slow to Whitehall Jn.(and Leeds Jn.,) Up & Down Goods & 2nd Goods line Kirkstall Jn.-Armley Canal Jn., Up & Down Goods Engine Shed Jn.-Waterloo Colliery Sidings.(Block signalling Hunslet Goods Jn.-Station Jn. No Block or Bell Station Jn.-South Jn.) 2nd Up Goods Wakefield Road-Stourton Jn., 2nd Up & Down Goods Stourton Down Sidings-Stourton Jn., 2nd Down Goods Stourton Jn.-Wakefield Road. At Armley station there was a Down "lie-by"(refuge) siding holding 29 wagons.

ALONG THE MIDLAND

Above: On the outskirts of Leeds, 4F 0-6-0 No. 44044 heads a train of empty mineral wagons south along the Midland line through Woodlesford station on 6th November 1960. The hoarding on the right proclaims the fine beers of Bentley's Yorkshire Brewery which was situated next to the line just after the station and was served by a private siding. The 1956 Stations Handbook listed Woodlesford as able to handle all classes of freight and equipped with a 10 ton crane but goods facilities were withdrawn on 27th April 1964. The station was reduced to an unstaffed halt on 4th January 1970 but remains open in 2009, though all buildings have gone.
P.B. Booth/Neville Stead collection

Below: It is 29th April 1962 and work has started on the new marshalling yard at Stourton but it would never be completed. The bridge is being built to carry the East & West Yorkshire Union Railway from Ardsley over new arrival lines into the yard.
The Bedford Dormobile van is every bit as classic as the 8F 2-8-0 heading south past Rothwell Haigh signal box with a special train of concrete beams, almost certainly for the new bridge. *Robert Anderson*

Above: Stourton looking south from Wakefield Road bridge on 20th May 1962. From left are the wagon shops and sidings, No.2 Up Goods line, No.1 Up Goods, Up and Down main lines, No. 1 Down Goods, No. 2 Down Goods, Down sidings, motive power depot, and Wakefield Road signal box. The Up yard, which handled general freight traffic, is beyond the wagon shops sidings and the Down yard, which handled coal traffic, is beyond the signal gantry. Wakefield Road box was abolished per the 4-weekly notice issued on 15th February 1969. In 2009 the Freightliner terminal and a steel depot occupy the site of the Down yard while a stone terminal, formerly at Balm Road, is on the left. *Peter Rose*

Below: No. 11001 was one of BR's earliest diesel shunters, being built at Ashford Works in 1950 and, although of Bullied Southern Railway design, it had a spell at Stourton c1952 following repairs at the Hunslet works. Designed for shunting and transfer work, the 0-6-0 was fitted with a Davey Paxman 12 cylinder engine rated at 500hp producing a maximum tractive effort of 33,500lbs when in low gear. Seen in Stourton sidings complete with stencilled 20B shedcode, it eventually returned to the Southern Region, being allocated to Norwood Junction. *Tom Greaves*

Yorkshire Copper Works Siding, Stourton. Wagons must not be loose shunted into the Yorkshire Copper Works Siding, and any wagons left standing on the bank must have all brakes pinned down. *BR Eastern Region Northern Area Sectional Appendix 1969*

18

January 1954: A4 No.60033 *Seagull* damaged in a collision at Copley Hill.

16.2.54: After visiting Don-caster Works, Carlisle A3 60093 *Coronach* works to Leeds on the 8.15pm braked goods from King's Cross.

25.10.54: 'Scot' 46112 *Sherwood Forester* works the 2-coach 9.33am Bradford -Leeds City local. 46113 *Cameronian* is on a 4-coach mid-day local.

29.8.57: K3 2-6-0 61972(31B) arrives at Leeds Central with the Harrogate portion of the Yorkshire Pullman.

A general view of Stourton shed which was coded 20B until being transferred from the London Midland Region to the North Eastern Region in 1956 when it became 55B.

As with any freight shed, the yard could be packed out with engines on a Sunday and this was the case on 20th May 1962 when the yard was well filled with engines typical of the types to be found there. From left, are a line-up of 4F 0-6-0s, a contingent of 350hp 0-6-0 diesel shunters, and a "Crab" 2-6-0 keeping the coal stage stocked up. The flat-roofed single-turntable roundhouse is in the background, left of the coal stage. Stourton shed was closed in January 1967 and its engines shared between Holbeck, Royston and Normanton. *Peter Rose*

STEAM LOCOMOTIVES ALLOCATED TO STOURTON, JANUARY 1957

Johnson 1F 0-6-0T: 41661/41797; Ivatt Class 4 2-6-0: 43014/44; Johnson 3F 0-6-0: 43392/456/579/681/737; Midland 4F 0-6-0: 43851/71/931/87; LMS 4F 0-6-0: 44028/94/153/238/335/467/570/584/586; Midland 3F 0-6-0T: 47249; LMS 3F 0-6-0T: 47271/443/463/538/589/632/640; 8F 2-8-0: 48126/276/311/358/443/537/622/641/652/703/721; Johnson 2F 0-6-0: 58136. Total: 42.

LOCOMOTIVES ALLOCATED TO STOURTON, NOVEMBER 1966

Ivatt Class 4 2-6-0: 43084/96/102/140; Class 5 4-6-0: 45080/211/428; 8F 2-8-0: 48084/093/126/130/622/641/703; BR Class 3 2-6-0: 77000/3/4; BR 350hp 0-6-0 diesel: D3294-96/454/654/55. Total: 23

Above: Midland Railway 4F 0-6-0 No. 43968 and shunter take a welcome break from their toils in Stourton yard during the sweltering heat of the 1959 summer. The 4F, seen at 3.9pm on Saturday 5th September, is paired with an old Johnson tender. *Robert Anderson*

Below: Doncaster-based O2 2-8-0 No. 63973, reversing onto Stourton shed on the same day. Had it travelled there via the East & West Yorkshire Union line which linked Stourton with the Doncaster-Leeds line at Ardsley? *Robert Anderson*

Above: 4F 0-6-0 No. 44584 brings what looks to be a trip working to Stourton under Pepper Road bridge and past Hunslet South signal box on 7th May 1963. Hunslet Down yard is visible through the arch on the left and the gravity shunt neck, known locally as "Rhubarb End," is on the left along with the three reception roads. *Peter Rose*

Below: It is 3rd October 1967 and the age of main line steam in Yorkshire is very nearly at an end but Carlisle Kingmoor 9F 2-10-0 No. 92218 shows it can still do a useful job. Having just come under the bridge carrying the Beeston Junction to Hunslet East branch, it threads Hunslet Down Yard reception sidings with special working 8Z71 conveying a heavy load of steel for Carlisle. The diesel shunter is on the gravity shunt neck. *Robert Anderson*

Looking towards Leeds at Hunslet Down yard with 8F 2-8-0 No. 48274 in charge of a trip working to Stourton on 7th May 1963. Hunslet Down yard dealt with general freight and the Up yard with coal. After many years out of use, the Down sidings were refurbished in 2004 for stabling coal wagons used by Freightliner Heavy Haul whose Midland Road traction depot occupies the site of the Up yard, just visible on the right. A 350hp shunter is on the gravity shunt neck which was removed during remodelling in 1980. *Peter Rose*

LEEDS PRIVATE SIDINGS 1956

Bramley Engineering Co.(via Fitton's Siding)
Brotherton & Co. Chemical Works(via North Eastern Gas
    Board, Meadow Lane Siding)
Carr & Co. Ltd.(via Tunstall & Co.'s siding)
Clayton, Son & Co. Ltd. - Dartmouth Siding, Moor End Works
   (via Middleton Broom Colliery line)
Clayton, Son & Co. Ltd. - Pepper Road Siding
Deighton's Patent Flue & Tube Works(via Clayton, Son & Co.'s
   Pepper Road siding)
Denison, S. & Son Ltd., Hunslet Moor Siding
   (via Middleton Broom Colliery line)
Elliot, Douglas & Co.'s Siding, Wellington Street North
Fitton's Siding, Hunslet East
Fowler & Co.'s Siding, Hunslet Lane
Gibson & Son's Power House Siding, Marsh Lane
Gooddall, Clayton & Co.(via Clayton's Pepper Road siding)
Holloway Bros.(London) Ltd., Waterloo Main Colliery
Hudswell, Clarke & Co., Hunslet.
Hunslet Engine Co., Hunslet
Joy, Edward & Sons Ltd.(via NEGB Meadow Lane siding)
King, J. & Co.(Leeds) Ltd. (via Middleton Broom Colliery line)
Leeds Briquette Works, Kirkstall
Leeds City Coal & Coke Co., Marsh lane & Hunslet East
Leeds City Coal & Coke Co., Waterloo Main Colliery
Leeds Corporation Cattle Market Siding, Copley Hill

Leeds Highways Dept., Wellington Street North
Liversidge, J. & Sons, Pepper Road.
McLaren, J. H. Ltd., Hunslet lane
Marshall, Thos. & Son Ltd., Wellington Street North
Middleton Fireclay Co. Ltd. Middleton Broom Colliery
Ministry of Supply, Monk Bridge Iron Works
National Coal Board, Middleton Broom Colliery
National Coal Board, Waterloo Main Colliery
National Cold Stores, Pepper Road, Hunslet
Nicholson J. & Sons Chemical Works, Hunslet
North Eastern Gas Board, Meadow Lane, Hunslet
North Eastern Gas Board, New Wortley
Northern Asphalt Co.'s Roofing Works, Cardigan Road
Parkfield Foundry Co.(via Middleton Broom Colliery line)
Parkinson, Sir Lindsay & Co., Waterloo Main Colliery
Robinson & Birdsall(via Middleton Broom Colliery line)
Tunstall & Co.'s Siding, Whitehall Road
Union Cold Storage Co. Ltd., Hunslet Lane
Wagon Repairs Ltd.(via Middleton Broom Colliery line)
Whitaker, Michael, Ltd.(via Middleton Broom Colliery line)

TRAINS AND LOCOMOTIVES READY TO DEPART FROM STEELWORKS AND TURNTABLE SIDINGS - South Junction. A plunger is provided near to the outlet signal from the sidings to enable the fireman to advise the signalman at Hunslet South Junction that his train or locomotive is ready to depart. *BR Eastern Region Northern Area Sectional Appendix, 1969.*

Right: By the 1970s, one of the private sidings at Hunslet was in the ownership of Miles Druce Sheet Processing Ltd. Their loco was Barclay 0-4-0 diesel works No. 341 of 1940 which appeared out of use when photographed on 20th April 1977. Hunslet Down sidings are in the background. *Adrian Booth*

Below: In the early years of preservation, the Middleton Railway, which formerly ran to Broom Colliery, still carried freight to several private sidings. Here, pioneer 0-6-0 diesel shunter *John Alcock*, built by the nearby Hunslet Engine Co. in 1932, works No. 1697 and LMS No. 7401, assists ex-NER 0-4-0T No. 1310(LNER class Y7) on freight duty at Hunslet Balm Road, the Middleton's connection with the Midland line. Ahead of them on the left was the Acme siding before Moor Road where the line crosses the route of the original 1758 incline which was abandoned in 1881. Immediately after that was the junction with the line from Hunslet coal depot, which originally went to the riverside, and a collection of sidings serving Clayton's, King's, Birdsell's, and Denison's. *Tom Greaves*

23

Above: Hunslet station on 29th August 1961. The driver of Bradford Manningham's Johnson ex-Midland Railway 3F 0-6-0 No. 43586 will have whistled for a water stop at Hunslet when passing Kirkstall Junction, subsequent box to box bell signals conveying the appropriate routing code.

Purely a passenger station, Hunslet was served by stopping trains to Sheffield, Cudworth, Knottingley and Leeds City. It closed on 13th June 1960 and the station buildings on the overbridge had already been removed by the time of this picture. *Peter Rose*

Left: Hunslet's alternative rail passenger service. Leeds tramways 4-wheel car No. 275 at Hunslet terminus in 1955. *C. Banks collection/Colour -Rail IR247*

Right: The Hunslet Engine Co. had a great railway presence in Leeds until its Jack Lane works closed in the 1990s. Among its many products were pioneering diesel shunting locomotives. This diminutive 4-wheel diesel mechanical loco, works No. 1850, seen at the works on 28th June 1970, was built in 1937. A Hudson Hunslet, it was built in association with Hudson's of Gildersome. *Adrian Booth*

Below: Examples of oldest and newest Hunslet steam locos top and tail this line at their creator's works on 21st November 1969. At the front is 87 year-old 0-4-0ST works No. 299 - with the name *Jenny* chalked on its smokebox door - while at the back is Austerity 0-6-0ST works No. 3885, just five years old and at that time one of the very last British built standard gauge steam locos. Between them is ex-BR Class 05 0-6-0 diesel No. D2617(works No. 5666/61,) bought as a source of spares when withdrawn by BR in 1967. *Adrian Booth*

Above: A busy scene inside the Hunslet assembly shop on 26th June 1985 with mine locos under construction or repair in the foreground, and a shunting loco and two metro trains behind them. *Adrian Booth*

Below: On 19th September 1984, works Nos. 9240 and 9241, were among 3ft gauge diesel hydraulic locos under construction for the Irish Turf Board(Bord Na Mona.) *Adrian Booth*

SHORT MEMORIES

September 1957: V2 60840 (64A) works the Harrogate portion of the Yorkshire Pullman into Central on the 9th, Black Five 45225(26A) on the 10th, Standard Class 5 73170 (50A) on the 11th, Jubilees 45702 *Colossus* and 45671 *Prince Rupert* (both 26A) on the 12th & 13th respectively, and Standard 5 73163(50A) on the 14th.

24.7.59: Trafford Park Britannia 70042 *Lord Roberts* arrives at City on the 11.36am local from Sheffield and leaves on the 4.11pm return.

5.4.60: Clan Pacific 72008 *Clan Macleod* on Holbeck shed.

15.5.60 Britannia *70050 Firth of Clyde*(66A) powers the 7.15am York-Leeds - part of a diagram which includes the Swansea-York mail.

July 1960: Leeds crews begin crew training from Neville Hill to the Settle & Carlisle line with English Electric Type 4s and empty stock.

19-21.7.60: A Trans-Pennine unit makes maiden runs Leeds-Liverpool and Leeds-Hull. The Liverpool run is worked by Farnley men and the Hull run by Neville Hill men.

Sept. 1960: A deceleration of ECML services due to modernisation work at Peterborough hits Leeds-King's Cross trains. The 10am from Leeds is 19 minutes slower, the Up White Rose 16 minutes slower, and the Up Queen of Scots takes 15 minutes longer, 32 minutes more than in 1939!

Above: A much quieter Hunslet assembly shop in March 1992 showing works shunter No.3, an 0-6-0 diesel hydraulic built by Hunslet in 1979, works No. 8976. In the background is another Hunslet 0-6-0 diesel belonging to Powergen.
During its 130-year history, the Hunslet works in Leeds built nearly 9,5 00 locomotives for UK and overseas customers, including industrial and main line shunters and mines locomotives. *Stephen Chapman*

Below: One of the last major orders for the Hunslet works was the Class 323 electric multiple units for British Rail services in Greater Manchester and the West Midlands, seen here under construction in March 1992. Built under the company brand Hunslet TPL, they suffered highly publicised technical problems and delayed entry into service which combined with the decline of Hunslet's major customer, the coal industry, to bring about the company's downfall. The works closed in 1995, shortly after the 323 order was completed. The Hunslet Engine Company itself survived but not in Jack Lane, having been initially bought by mining equipment specialists Qualter Hall of Barnsley, while in 2009 it is part of Staffordshire-based LH Group Services Ltd. *Stephen Chapman*

Originally the terminus of the North Midland Railway from Derby, complete with passenger station and engine shed, the vast Hunslet Lane yard survived for over 130 years. Transferred from BR to the road-oriented National Carriers in 1972, it survived until the early 1980s by which time it saw very little rail traffic. It was listed in the 1956 Handbook of Stations as being equipped with cranage capacity up to 40 tons and able to handle all classes of goods traffic.

Right: Viewed from the yard's own signal box on 9th May 1963 are, from left: the old NMR engine house, the pit and water column used by the yard pilots, the bonded store, Goliath overhead crane, the main goods warehouse, and sidings which throughout the yard totalled 40. A siding to Meadow Lane gas works went off to the left while sidings went into John Fowler's steam plough and engine works from a turntable in a siding to the far right. So busy was Hunslet Lane that several locomotives can be seen, including two of Holbeck's 204hp diesel shunters and a pair of Stourton 4Fs waiting to collect their trains. *Peter Rose*

The BR Eastern Region Northern Area Sectional Appendix 1969 stated that the Hunslet Lane goods yard branch was 555 yards long from Hunslet Goods Junction signal box to Hunslet Goods Yard signal box. It had no block signalling and the maximum permitted speed was 15mph. Additional lines were the Wall Side Arrival and Wall Side Departure lines. It also stated that steam locomotives were permitted to assist departing freight trains over the Main and Wall Side departure lines on condition that they were not coupled to the train.

Hunslet Lane Goods Arrivals and departures as shown in the winter 1959/60 working timetable

1.40am class F to Crofton Hall
3.40am MX 4.48pm class C from Bristol
6.54am SX 6.5am class C from Huddersfield
6.55pm class D to Keighley
7.20pm SX class K to Stourton Up Sidings
7.25-7.42pm SX 6.45pm Bradford-Dock Junction class C *Reverse and engine change*
7.50pm class K to Copley Hill
8.20pm class K to Stourton Up Sidings
9.30pm class K to Stourton Up Sidings

Left: This LNER Pacific tender, reputed to be from A4 No. 60026 *Miles Beevor*, was found in the yard at Hunslet Lane on 6th May 1975. It was fitted with buffers and drawhook on the front, enabling it to be towed about. *Peter Rose*

Below: Stanier Class 5 4-6-0 No. 44897 propels its train, the 18.25 to Carlisle via Bradford Valley, out of Hunslet Lane and on to the main line at Hunslet Goods Junction on 12th July 1967. No. 44897 worked tender first to Bradford from where it was chimney first to Carlisle. Hunslet Goods Junction signal box on the right ceased to be a Block Post per the 4-weekly notice issued on 7th June 1969. *Brian Myland.*

Above: On 9th May 1963, Stanier Class 5 4-6-0 No. 44841 from Saltley shed, Birmingham, restarts its Up(probably a Carlisle to Washwood Heath) class 5 express freight from signals at Hunslet Goods Junction. It had been held to let the Hunslet Lane-London fitted freight have preference. *Peter Rose*

Below: Deputising for an unavailable diesel, Class 5 4-6-0 No. 44944, also from Saltley, passes the loco coal/gas oil sidings for Holbeck motive power depot with the 7.40am Bristol-Bradford Forster Square at 1.44pm on 17th February 1962. *Robert Anderson*

Above: Engine Shed Junction takes its name from the adjacent Holbeck motive power depot, to the left of the picture. Here, Jubilee No. 45622 *Nyasaland* of 14B Kentish Town shed looks in fine fettle as she heads for London with the Thames-Clyde Express at 2.33pm on 17th February 1962 while deputising for an unavailable "Peak" diesel. The signal box ceased to be a Block Post per the 4-weekly notice issued on 7th June 1969. *Robert Anderson*

Below: In August 1955 Holbeck shed's massive coal plant was out of action and a barely adequate vintage relief steam crane was brought in for coaling locos. No. 45565 *Victoria* is the Jubilee being replenished at 2pm on the 10th. *Robert Anderson*

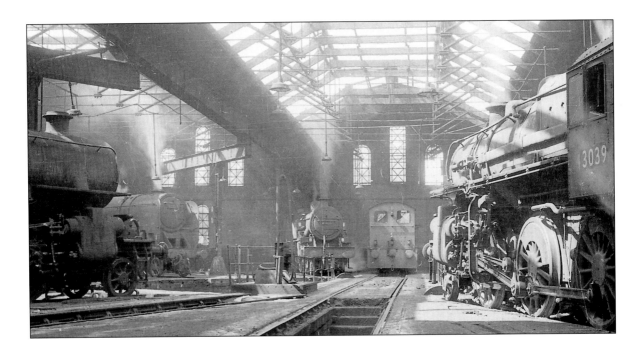

Holbeck was "top shed" in the Leeds motive power district of BR's London Midland Region, coded 20A until 1956 when the district was transferred to the North Eastern Region and Holbeck became 55A. Under the computerized TOPS system in the 1970s it became HO. Facilities included a large roundhouse with stalls radiating from two turntables capable of accommodating 44 engines, an adjacent repair shop containing three straight roads, and a mechanical coaling plant equipped to coal two locomotives simultaneously.

The workload for Holbeck's engines was mixed passenger, shunting and freight but the role for which it is best remembered was providing express passenger engines for the Midland Main line both south and north of Leeds, notably the Jubilee and Royal Scot 4-6-0s, a selection of Britannia Pacifics, and the ex-LNER A3 Pacifics drafted in for the Carlisle line in 1960/61.

Holbeck closed to steam on 30th September 1967. The roundhouse and coaling plant were demolished in 1969/70, the site of the coaling plant being appropriately taken by a two-road diesel fuelling shed while the repair shed had been utilized for diesel maintenance since before the end of steam. Following the combination of City and Central stations, Holbeck came to service and maintain locomotives used on all services from Leeds including those to King's Cross which brought Deltics to the depot. The full High Speed Train timetable on the East Coast line in 1978 saw the need for passenger locomotives much reduced and Holbeck lost its main line allocation. It continued to service and refuel visiting and outbased locomotives until the mid-1990s when it finally closed, becoming a depot for engineers' on-track plant, the role it still fulfils in 2009.

Above: The inside of a large roundhouse, its engines brooding around the turntables, was breathtaking, inspirational and unforgettable. The picture above shows Holbeck's roundhouse in 1963 with two Ivatt Class 4 2-6-0s, a 9F 2-10-0, a Fowler Class 4 2-6-4T and a Drewry 204hp 0-6-0 diesel shunter(locally nicknamed "Sugar Puffs") ranged around one of its two turntables. *Arthur Chester*

STEAM LOCOMOTIVES ALLOCATED TO HOLBECK JANUARY 1957

Stanier Class 3 2-6-2T: 40140/69/93; 2P 4-4-0: 40491/552/690; 4P Compound 4-4-0: 41068/71/94/1100; Ivatt Class 2 2-6-2T: 41267; Fowler Class 4 2-6-4T: 42377; Hughes-Fowler 6P5F 2-6-0: 42771/4/95/98; Ivatt Class 4 2-6-0: 43039/117; Midland 4F 0-6-0: 43968; LMS 4F 0-6-0: 44044/55/207; Stanier Class 5 4-6-0: 44662/826/28/49/52/53/54/57/943/83/5273/428; Stanier Class 5 4-6-0 with Caprotti valve gear: 44753/54/55/56/57; Class 6P "Jubilee" 4-6-0: 45562 *Alberta*/45564 *New South Wales*/45565 *Victoria*/ 45566 *Queensland*/45568 *Western Australia*/45569 *Tasmania*/45573 *Newfoundland*/45589 *Gwalior*/45597 *Barbados*/45605 *Cyprus*/45608 *Gibraltar*/45619 *Nigeria*/45639 *Raleigh*/45658 *Keyes*/45659 *Drake*/45675 *Hardy*/45694 *Bellerophon*/45739 *Ulster;* Class 7P "Royal Scot" 4-6-0: 46103 *Royal Scots Fusilier*/46108 *Seaforth Highlander*/ 46109 *Royal Engineer*/46112 *Sherwood Forester*/46113 *Cameronian*/46117 *Welsh Guardsman*/46133 *The Green Howards*/46145 *The Duke of Wellington's Regt.(West Riding)*; Ivatt Class 2 2-6-0: 46453/93/98; Midland 3F 0-6-0T: 47254; LMS 3F 0-6-0T: 47418/20/36; 8F 2-8-0: 48067/104/57/58/59/283/399/454; BR Standard Class 5 4-6-0: 73010/45/53/66/69. Total: 85

LOCOMOTIVES ALLOCATED TO HOLBECK APRIL 1965

Fairburn Class 4 2-6-4T: 42139/45/271; Fowler Class 4 2-6-4T: 42394; Stanier Class 4 2-6-4T: 42622; Ivatt Class 4 2-6-0: 43039/117/124/130; Stanier Class 5 4-6-0: 44824/28/52/53/54/57/983/5063/75/79/204/11/73; Class 6P "Jubilee" 4-6-0: 45573 *Newfoundland*/45593 *Kolhapur*/45608 *Gibraltar*/45626 *Seychelles*/45658 *Keyes*/45660 *Rooke*/45661 *Vernon*/45664 *Nelson*/45675 *Hardy*/45697 *Achilles*/45739 *Ulster*; 8F 2-8-0: 48104/57/58/283/399/454/542; BR/Sulzer "Peak" Type 4: D14-32; Brush Type 4: D1570/1/2/3; BR/Gardner 204hp 0-6-0: D2074; Drewry 204hp 0-6-0: D2248/67/71/2/3; 350hp 0-6-0: D3235/380. Total: 71

Above: 4-4-0s of Midland and LMS origin were staple passenger power at Holbeck until bigger engines came along and still had work to do until displaced by diesels in the late 1950s. Ex-Midland 2P No. 40552's working life is over and it awaits its fate stored on the snow-plough road at 8.10pm on 6th June 1960, the month it was withdrawn. *Robert Anderson*

Below: Classic Midland during the transition to BR. Johnson 3P No. 40728, belonging to a class introduced by the Midland Railway in 1901, stands by Holbeck's coal plant on 18th September 1948. *Neville Stead collection*

Above: The last of Holbeck's Royal Scots were transferred away, mainly to Low Moor, at the end of the summer 1961 timetable when they were displaced by new BR/Sulzer "Peak" Type 4 diesels. But the diesels were plagued by failures and unavailability so no less than nine "Scots" had to be brought back in summer 1962, all but one staying at Holbeck until withdrawn from service in November/December. Here, No. 46113 *Cameronian* uses No.1 turntable in Holbeck shed on 4th August 1962. It was finally withdrawn in December and, along with some of the others, put into store at Neville Hill. *Peter Rose*

Below: The BR Standard "Clan" Pacifics were not common visitors to Leeds but were not unknown. No. 72006 *Clan Mackenzie*, displaying a 68A Carlisle Kingmoor shedplate, rests at Holbeck in the mid-1950s. *Neville Stead collection*

Above: Just a bit rarer than the Clans! Southern Region Merchant Navy class Pacific No. 35012 *United States Line* arrives at Holbeck shed at 7.12pm on 12th June 1964 after running light from London's Nine Elms depot - complete with Nine Elms crew - to work the next day's Railway Correspondence & Travel Society "Solway Ranger" railtour. *Robert Anderson*

Below: In the diesel era, the BR/Sulzer "Peak" Type 4s - later Class 45s - were synonymous with Holbeck which had a sizeable allocation for Midland Main Line, Cross-Country and Carlisle work. Four of the class - D130 at the front - are seen standing outside the straight repair shop, by then utilized as a diesel depot, in 1963. *Arthur Chester*

LOCOMOTIVES ALLOCATED TO HOLBECK SEPTEMBER 1977

350hp 0-6-0 shunter: 08225/226/369/453/497-501/3/17/766; Brush Type 2: 31111/46/59/66/70/75/78/80/253/68/71/319/409/10; BR/Sulzer Type 4 "Peak:" 45001/2/6/7/9-22/24-32/34-36/38-41/43/47/48/53/61; Brush Type 4: 47425/6/34/57-62/518-22. Total: 79

On 9th October 1965 no less than seven Jubilees were noted on Holbeck. They were Nos. 45573, 45574, 45608, 45626, 45643, 45660 and 45697. Despite the approaching end of steam, 31 steam locos were noted on Holbeck on **5th July 1967**, including the three Jubilees 45562 *Alberta,* 45593 *Kolhapur* and 45697 *Achilles.*

Above: Jubilee No. 45608 *Gibraltar,* begrimed and minus nameplates, looks very forlorn as she simmers on the snowplough(No.6) road on a dismal 1st August 1965 as Farnley Class 5 No. 45080 pounds over the Wessie viaduct with a Blackpool excursion. No. 45626 *Seychelles* is on No.5 road and the breakdown crane on No.4. *Gibraltar* was withdrawn the following month and *Seychelles* in November. *Peter Rose*

Below: Inside the murky depths of Holbeck's roundhouse in October 1966 with Class 5 4-6-0 No. 44662 flanked by 8Fs 48104 and the prototype for the Hornby Dublo 3-rail model, No. 48158. *Jack Wild/ Stephen Chapman archive*

Above: Flowerpower? Forget it! As if anyone needed reminding, summer 1967 was really about the exploits of Holbeck's three remaining Jubilees on Carlisle expresses.

Above: The beautifully turned-out trio, 45697 *Achilles*, now-preserved 45593 *Kolhapur,* and 45562 *Alberta* line up for a family photo after being prepared for the remarkable summer ahead during which they became BR's last active steam express passenger engines.

Right: *Kolhapur* exudes majesty as she bathes in the sunshine outside Holbeck shed.

Both Tom Greaves

As Leeds traction engineer, Tom Greaves was largely responsible for the Jubilees' extended lease of life in summer 1967. He revealed to Railway Memories just how they came to be on front line express work so late in the steam era: "We needed six good locos for cover and specials in addition to the remaining diagrams. I also promised co-operation with the RCTS to cover some of the Saturday specials. We undertook a review of about 20 Class 5s and also considered the Jubilees. Tyres, cylinders and frame condition being the criteria.

"The Holbeck team were very enthusiastic and I got on well with shed master Ted Geeson who was a man of tremendous strengths. His mechanical foreman was Freddy Butts who worked very hard.

"The 5xs[Jubilees] were more problematic [than the Black Fives] as their Achilles Heel was the channel joints blowing when they reached higher mileage. Some new bolts were fitted to try and minimise the problem but towards the end, *Alberta* in particular became very bad. Geoff Wilson and the inspectorate also gave me great help and enthusiasm, hence the line-up for a photo-shoot of the three 5X ladies."

Above: Also smartened up for summer 1967 was "Black Five" No. 45428, which was stand-by for Jubilee *Alberta* when she worked the Royal Train conveying the Duke of Edinburgh to Nidd Bridge and Ripon on 30th May. No. 45428 was subsequently preserved and became the last steam loco to go off Holbeck shed when on 24th August 1968, 11 months after the shed closed to steam, she left under her own power for a new home at Tyseley. This view by Tom Greaves of 45428 when she was rolled out after being bulled up illustrates the scale of the roundhouse which within three years would have disappeared.

Below: En-route from Rotherham to preservation on the Keighley & Worth Valley Railway in 1967, ex-Midland 1F 0-6-0T No. 41708 needed attention at Holbeck shed where it is seen up on blocks. *Tom Greaves*

Tom Greaves reveals why he chose 45428 for a special paint job in spring 1967: "When I took over Leeds it was my first opportunity to have a division where the LMS was in the majority, with Farnley, Low Moor and Holbeck.

"Before I went there, there had been a degree of open warfare between the divisional offices but the integration of Leeds, Wakefield and York offered new opportunities.

"There were still a significant number of steam workings and I always had two objectives, the first being to have a Black Five in similar condition to a pair I viewed as an enthusiast during a visit to Preston in my early days as a premium apprentice at Doncaster. I was determined to have one painted black with no colour relief other than numbers and buffer beam but with polished steel buffers, cylinder covers and smokebox fittings. Freddy Butts did a splendid job on 5428 but in his enthusiasm added red boiler bands which had to be removed. The advance information of Prince Philip's visit offered the justification for a bit of bulling up as it would be a brave railwayman who criticized our effort for such an event."

Contrasting visitors to Holbeck.

Right: In a truly woebegone state, minus its front numberplate and with the shed code 8C (Speke Junction) chalked on its smokebox door, former Crosti-boilered 9F 2-10-0 No. 92025 is replenished by Holbeck's coal hopper in 1967.

Built in 1927 of reinforced concrete, the twin-hoppered plant stood 120ft high. *Tom Greaves*

Below: In that same last full year of steam, preserved Western Region Castle class 4-6-0 No. 7029 *Clun Castle* brings a sparkle to Holbeck roundhouse and hints at the future shape of main line steam.

Great Western engines were out of gauge in this part of the world so No. 7029 had to undergo gauging trials before being allowed to work a series of railtours in 1967.

With traction inspector Mitchell in the cab keeping an eye on the photographer, she moves off the turntable at 09.50 prior to working a gauging special to Carcroft(Doncaster) and Calder Bridge(Wakefield) on 22nd August 1967. *Robert Anderson*

The changing shape of Holbeck.
Left: The seemingly indestructible giant coal plant is felled by explosives on 18th May 1969 - the second attempt.

Below: Awaiting its destruction, the massive bulk of the roundhouse, cold and empty, seen from beneath the Viaduct Line at the junction of Sweet Street West and Bridge Road on 25th February 1969. *Both Robert Anderson*

Bottom: Holbeck on 19th February 1993, in its final form and with its demise as a locomotive depot not far away. Class 47 locomotives and diesel multiple units, some stored, occupy the yard while in the centre is the fuelling shed built on the site of the coaling plant. The viaduct stands disused, while Engine Shed Junction is considerably slimmed down.
Stephen Chapman

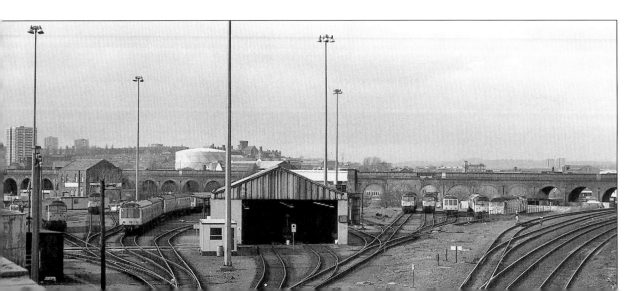

Above: Royal Scot 4-6-0 No. 46148 *The Manchester Regiment* brings the northbound Thames-Clyde Express under the Viaduct Line near Water Lane and takes the curve to Leeds City on 20th March 1961. The lines from Engine Shed Junction to Whitehall Junction are in the foreground.

Below: Coming the other way on a typically wet bank holiday Monday 5th August 1961 is Crewe South Jubilee 4-6-0 No. 45644 *Howe*, utilized by Holbeck for an Up express. Leeds City Junction is in the background and the Viaduct Line on the right. The semaphore signals have gone but for the two shunt signals on the right, the top one for City North and the other for South, memorably used when Holbeck men reversed the 2.53pm Heysham parcels into South to attach vans which included the fish from Hull. *Both Peter Rose*

Left: Whitehall station, a temporary halt set up on the then single track Engine Shed Jn.-Whitehall Jn. line for use by certain passenger services unable to access Leeds City during reconstruction work in 2001. *Stephen Chapman*

Centre and bottom: Whitehall Junction on 1st March 1967. Britannia Pacific No. 70014 *Iron Duke* on a class 8 goods to Hunslet(below) passes Black Fives 45012 and 44726 which were being towed by 45219 from Carlisle to Draper's yard at Hull for scrapping when when one of 44726's tender wheels derailed, damaging signalling equipment with resulting chaos. And(bottom) looking west towards the junction with, from left, sidings into Whitehall goods yard, Whitehall Jn. signal box, the Engine Shed Jn. line, and the Black Fives on the line to City station. *Both Robert Anderson*

Above: Stanier Class 5 4-6-0 No. 44727 which, like 44726 on the previous page, was one of those introduced in 1949 with a steel firebox, accelerates the 14.20 Leeds-Heysham parcels away from Whitehall Junction on Friday 10th February 1967. To the right of the signal box can be see the big warehouse at Whitehall goods yard. *Both pictures on this page by Robert Anderson*

Below: Looking west over the former Holbeck Low Level station at 17.40 on 16th April 1967 as LNER K4 No. 3442 *The Great Marquess* waits to reverse an Epsom College Railway Society special from Stockport via East Lancashire off the Shipley line in order to access the Geldard curve and Leeds Central. One of the former Holbeck roundhouses and Geldard Junction signal box are on the right.

It is hard to believe nowadays that there was ever a station here with both high and low level platforms. Both levels were known as just Holbeck until 1st March 1951, when the GN platforms were renamed High Level and the Midland-North Eastern joint(opened 1862 to replace separate Midland and NE stations) became Low Level. They all closed on 7th July 1958 and the shorter Low Level platform between the fast lines removed. In summer 1957, Low Level saw 11 daily departures to City station, seven to Bradford, four to Ilkley via Otley, two to Skipton via Ilkley, two to Northallerton and one each to Ripon, Thirsk, West Hartlepool, Harrogate and Newcastle.

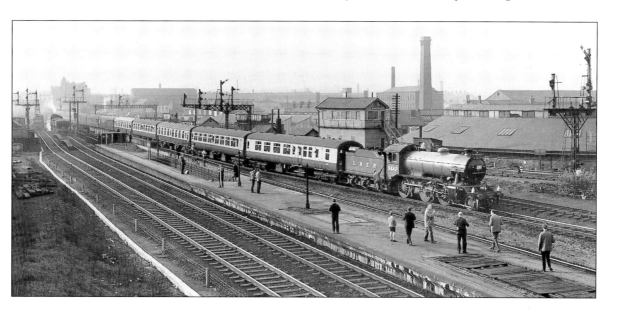

Above: Compound 4-4-0 No. 41196 approaches Whitehall Junction with an early 1950s Morecambe-Leeds stopper. It has just passed Holbeck Low Level while the high level station can be seen on the bridge. *J.W. Haigh/Neville Stead collection*

Below: Having just past Holbeck Low Level, Jubilee No. 45573 *Newfoundland* storms away from Leeds with the 07.25 Leicester to Gourock Creative Tourist Agents Conference special at 11.07 on 10th July 1965. It will combine at Hellifield with the 09.50 portion from Manchester. *Newfoundland* was withdrawn only a couple of months later. *Robert Anderson*
Armley Road coal drops are on the left and Wortley gas works sidings on the right. There are still four electrified lines here in 2009 but all else is gone and the railway looks very thin on the ground compared with this view.

Above: Fowler 2-6-4T No. 42394 passes Wortley NE box with the 08.50 Bradford Forster Square to St. Pancras on 7th July 1965. *Roy Wood/ Peter Rose colln.* Wortley gas works is on the left but with natural gas on its way, not for much longer.

Right: Midland 3F 0-6-0 No. 43476 emerges from Wellington Street goods and passes Geldard Junction box with a local trip in May 1952. The curve on the right rises up to Central station. Over the weekend 29th April-1st May 1967, the Down line was abandoned and the Up line converted to One Engine in Steam working to serve the High Level goods depot. *Peter Cookson/N. Stead colln.*

Trains passing Wortley Junction on the evening of 23.4.1945 *An extract from the train register by courtesy of Peter Rose*

Time	Line	Train description	Engine
7.2	Up Slow	LMS ordinary passenger	4P 4-4-0 No.1040
7.9	Up Slow	LMS light engine	2F 0-6-0 No.3173
7.10	Up NE Fast	LNE passenger	D20 4-4-0 No.1236
7.20	Down Fast	LMS ordinary passenger	5XP 4-6-0 No.5619
7.31	Up Fast/Slow	LMS class A goods	5F 2-6-0 No.2762
7.35	Up Slow	LMS class B goods	4F 0-6-0 No.4570
7.44	Up Fast/Slow	LMS class A goods	3F 0-6-0 No.3678
7.49	Up Fast	LMS stopping passenger	4P 4-4-0 No.932
7.54	Up Slow	LMS class B goods	8F 2-8-0 No.8647
7.54	Down Fast/NE	LNE passenger	D20 4-4-0 No.708
8.0	Down Slow	LMS light engine	8F 2--8-0 No.8358
8.5	Down Slow	LMS class B goods	4F 0-6-0 No.4094
8.10	Up Slow	LMS fitted goods	8F 2-8-0 No.8271
8.16	Down Fast	LMS express passenger	4P 4-4-0 No.1095
8.18	Up Fast/Slow	LMS class B goods	4F 0-6-0 No.3984

Time	Line	Train description	Engine
8.24	Up Fast/Slow	LMS mineral	4F 0-6-0 No.3998
8.24	Down Fast	LMS ordinary passenger	4P 4-4-0 No.1004
8.28	Up Fast/Slow	LMS stopping goods	3F 0-6-0 No.3778
8.34	Up Slow	LMS light engine	8F 2-8-0 No.8082
8.42	Up Slow	LMS class A goods	4P 4-4-0 No.1144
8.47	Up Slow	LMS light engine	4F 0-6-0 No.3904
8.49	Down Slow	LMS class B goods	3F 0-6-0 No.3678
9.0	Up Slow	LMS ordinary passenger	2P 2-4-2T No.10622
9.2	Down Slow	LMS fitted goods	5 4-6-0 No.4842
9.12	Down Fast	LMS ordinary passenger	2P 0-4-4T No.6400
9.17	Up NE/Fast	LNE passenger	V1 2-6-2T No. 415
9.29	Up Fast	LMS ordinary passenger	5XP 4-6-0 No.5538
9.40	Up NE/Fast	LNE goods	J39 0-6-0 No. 1473
9.42	Down Fast/NE	LNE passenger	D20 4-4-0 No.1236

Left: Having just passed through Armley Canal Road station, deplorably filthy Jubilee No. 45675 *Hardy* heads purposefully towards Kirkstall flyover with the 06.35 Birmingham-Glasgow at 10.43 on 24th July 1965. The train had been delayed by congestion at Leeds City South. Canal Road had closed just four months earlier on 22nd March during a Beeching cull of Leeds North West services.
Robert Anderson

Below: Kirkstall flyover was built when the line was widened to accommodate increased traffic created by the Settle & Carlisle. It avoided conflicting movements by taking the Fast lines over the Slow lines.
B1 4-6-0 No. 61096 heads a lengthy and unidentified express along the Up Fast towards Leeds on 3rd July 1960. As 61096 carries a 41A Sheffield Darnall shedplate, it seems likely that the train is a Morecambe-Sheffield or Nottingham summer dated service. The Slow lines can be seen down below on the left. *Neville Stead collection*

Opposite: From late 1958 to August 1962 three Britannia Pacifics were allocated to Holbeck and mostly they worked the Midland line north of Leeds. On 26th June 1960, No. 70053 *Moray Firth* heads the northbound Thames-Clyde towards Calverley & Rodley.
P.B. Booth/Neville Stead collection

Left: Jubilee No. 45658 *Keyes* takes the lower level Slow lines at the flyover as it forges past Kirkstall power station with the 8.30am Glasgow to St. Pancras Easter Saturday extra at 1.26pm on 13th April 1963.
A Holbeck engine for its entire working life, *Keyes* clocked up the highest known Jubilee mileage of 1,728,870 from new to 12th June 1961 when records ceased. It was withdrawn on 13th September 1965 so may well have reached 2 million. *Robert Anderson*

Below: Though one was named *City of Leeds*, the Coronation Pacifics did not normally go there which presumably made Leeds an attractive choice of railtour itinery for this illustrious class in their final months. No. 46255 *City of Hereford* passes Kirkstall Junction with an Up Stephenson Locomotive Society special on 12th July 1964. *Roy Wood/Peter Rose colln.*

Above: Pretty well the very last BR steam action to be found in Leeds by 1968 was provided by the Heysham-Hunslet East oil trains, such as this one seen between Calverley & Rodley and Newlay & Horsforth at 16.00 on 25th August 1967, headed by 9F 2-10-0 No. 92212 with BR/Sulzer Type 2(Class 25) No. D5256 assisting.

The usual procedure was for the Class 25 to be detached in Kirkstall Goods Loop and run light to Holbeck depot, the 9F continuing with the train to Neville Hill sidings. There the 9F would detach and go to Neville Hill depot to turn and take water while two 350hp(Class 08) shunters took the tanks down the branch to Hunslet East, the 9F then working the empty tanks back home. *Robert Anderson*

Below: Lancaster-based Ivatt Class 4 2-6-0 No. 43113 has just passed Calverley & Rodley station with the combined 2.43pm Carnforth/2.46pm Morecambe-Leeds at 4.35 on 16th August 1961. *Robert Anderson* The 1956 Stations Handbook listed the goods yard on the left as being able to handle general goods and livestock only and equipped with 10-ton cranage, though the yard crane had clearly been dismantled by the time of this picture. The 4-platform passenger station, whose buildings can be seen on the overbridge, closed on 22nd March 1965 and the goods yard on 7th October 1968. The signal box from which this shot was taken, was abolished per the 4-weekly notice issued on 7th June 1969 as the Leeds power box continued to extend its area of control.

SHORT MEMORIES

October 1961: Royal Scots and Patriots remain regular power for the 11am Liverpool-Newcastle and 4.47pm return due to unavailability of Type 4 diesels. They are routed via Dewsbury to avoid the steeply graded New Line.

6.10.61: The 3.16pm Newcastle-Liverpool is delayed two hours when 46119 *Lancashire Fusilier* - deputising for an unavailable diesel - fails in Gildersome Tunnel. It is rescued by 'Super D' 0-8-0 No. 49034.

In September 1957 there were the following signal boxes(with distance from previous box) between Leeds City and Garforth: Leeds City East; Marsh Lane(1268yds.,) Neville Hill West(1255yds.,) Neville Hill East (1008yds.,) Killingbeck(1 mile 218yds.,) Cross Gates(1 mile 420yds.,) and Garforth(3 miles 129yds.)

Above: Like the Midland, the North Eastern reached Leeds from two opposing directions. At the east end of Leeds City South on 23rd June 1957, classic NER motive power, D20 4-4-0 No. 62387, waits to leave platform 15 with an RCTS railtour to the Ryedale lines and Whitby. Platform 16 is on the right, and the horse and vehicle dock right of that, hidden by 62387's train. The 1960s rebuild saw platforms 14 and 15 converted to through platforms 5 and 6 while No.16 became platform 4(today's No.7.) *Ken Hoole/N. Stead colln.*

Below: The Marsh Lane station pictured here replaced the Leeds & Selby terminus when the line was built along the viaducts to Leeds New station in 1869. Until closed with effect from 15th September 1958, Marsh Lane was served by a handful of trains between Leeds City and Wetherby, Harrogate, Micklefield, Selby, Hull and York. The station buildings are on the right as A3 No. 60072 *Sunstar* ambles through on its way to Neville Hill depot on 19th July 1961. *Roy Wood/Peter Rose collection*

Above: On 31st July 1961 Standard Class 5 4-6-0 No. 73162 hustles the 9.42am Leeds-Bridlington through Richmond Hill cutting - a 700-yard tunnel until opened out in the 1890s to accommodate extra tracks. This train called at intermediate stations to Selby and then ran via Market Weighton. On Saturdays 24th June to 26th August it continued to Filey Holiday Camp. *Peter Rose.*

Below: One mile 763 yards from Leeds City, the by then privately-owned A4 Pacific No. 60019 *Bittern* storms past Neville Hill West Junction at 08.11 on 12th November 1966 with an A4 Preservation Society special to Edinburgh via Hexham and Carlisle bearing The Waverley headboard. The lines in the right foreground lead into the depot while the branch to Hunslet East trails away to the left. *Robert Anderson*

The Hunslet East branch was shown by the 1969 BR Eastern Region Sectional Appendix as one mile 92 yards long with no block signalling. The maximum speed was 20mph. It is still used for stone and cement traffic in 2009 but has been singled.

The 1960 BR Sectional Appendix stated that more than one engine or train was allowed on the Hunslet East goods branch at a time subject to certain conditions including:

The first train...entering the branch in the morning must do so on the understanding that the line is only clear to the Stop Board opposite the shunter's box[in Hunslet Yard.] The driver must not go beyond this board until he receives instructions from the guard who must first receive the authority of the shunter.

After the first train has arrived... the shunter must arrange as soon as possible to have it drawn inside the Stop Board, and after the line has been cleared to the fouling point with the first siding connection beyond the Stop Board, the shunter must immediately advise the signalman at Neville Hill...that this has been done and give his name.

Should the Neville Hill signalman require a second train...to enter the branch, he must, after receiving an assurance from the Hunslet Yard shunter that the first train is inside the Stop Board verbally inform the driver that a train is already in Hunslet Yard, and that he must go cautiously forward as the line is only clear to the...Stop Board, and the signalman must not allow any other train to go into the branch until the shunter has advised him that the second train....is inside the Stop Board..

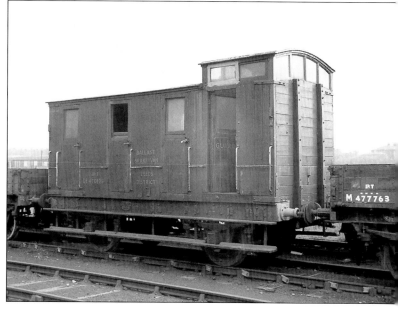

Above: Hunslet East was also used by the engineers who had a tip there. Among engineers wagons found there on 31st July 1961 was District Engineer's 20-ton ballast brake van No. DE470125. *Peter Rose*

Below: The extensive layout at Hunslet East in the 1930s. The 1956 Handbook of Stations listed the Great Northern depot at Hunslet East as being able to handle all classes of freight and equipped with maximum crane power of 10 tons. The North Eastern depot also had crane power of 10 tons but could only deal with livestock and "furniture vans, carriages, motor cars, portable engines and machines on wheels." Both closed with effect from 5th September 1966, but the line from Neville Hill lived on to serve new oil terminals operated by a new BR subsidiary called Oil Rail Terminals Ltd. The first opened in April 1965, deliveries including twice-weekly 1000-ton 22-wagon block trains from Immingham.

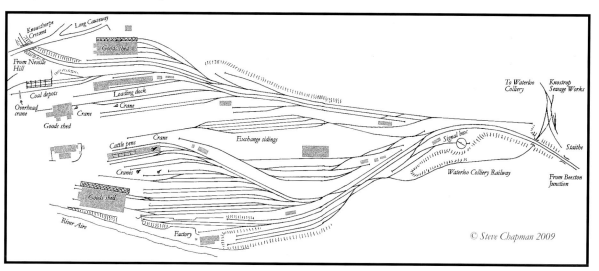

Class H trip workings serving Hunslet East(NE) were listed in the winter 1959/60 working timetable as 5.10 and 6.45am and 12.20, 1.10SO, and 4pm from Neville Hill, and 12.15SO, 12.50SX, 3 and 7.20PM to Neville Hill plus an untimed working between 6 and 7am. The York District Working of Local Freight and Mineral Trains book issued on 19th September 1955 showed Neville Hill Trip No. 3 booked to leave Neville Hill sidings at 5.20am and run class H to Hunslet East where it detached and picked up wagons as required before returning to Neville Hill. It then made trips as an untimed class K Neville Hill-Marsh Lane-Neville Hill-Cross Gates*-Barnbow Sidings*-Garforth*-Micklefield*-South Milford*-Gascoigne Wood-Garforth-Peckfield-Garforth-Cross Gates*-Neville Hill-Marsh Lane(class H)-Neville Hill. *When required. It also delivered and collected water cans as required.*

Inside Neville Hill roundhouse with Fairburn Class 4 2-6-4T No. 42196 on one of the two turntables on 20th July 1964. Behind are Ivatt Class 4 2-6-0 No. 43043 and A1 Pacific No. 60118. 42196 was one of the last steam engines allocated to Neville Hill. *Peter Rose*

Opened by the NER in 1904 to replace the old Leeds & Thirsk sheds at Holbeck, Neville Hill was coded 50B in the BR's North Eastern Region York District until January 1960 when it was taken into the Leeds District and re-coded 55H. Under the TOPS computer system introduced in the 1970s it became NL. The roundhouse was huge with three covered turntables plus an adjoining workshop with three straight roads. The roundhouse was extensively rebuilt and modernized in 1958, the turntables by then reduced to two.

It provided both passenger and goods engines for the North Eastern lines around Leeds, its allocation including everything from ex-NER tank engines to D49 4-4-0s and A3 Pacifics. In 1961 it became the first diesel locomotive depot in Leeds when it received "Peak" Type 4s(Class 45) D11-D18 new along with English Electric Type 4s(Class 40s) D345-348 to complement its growing fleet of multiple units, especially the Birmingham Railway Carriage & Wagon 4-car sets which later became Class 104 and Metro-Cammell sets which became classes 101 and 111. Also in 1961, the new Trans-Pennine DMUs were allocated to the Leeds shed because it had an engine drop pit, an essential maintenance facility which their eventual home, Hull Botanic Gardens, was not at first equipped with. Over the following year the number of "Peaks" grew, consisting of Nos. D14-32 along with the four Class 40s.

Neville Hill's future was as a DMU and carriage depot and the diesel locomotive allocation was only temporary until facilities were established at Holbeck, to where the Peaks had transferred by 1963, the Class 40s transferring to York. At that time Neville Hill was still a steam shed but its allocation was dwindling. Its A3s had all gone by the end of 1963 but in July it had received four A1s, which remained on its books until withdrawn in October 1965. Neville Hill finally closed to steam in June 1966 when its last half dozen steam locos were shared out between Normanton, Low Moor and Holbeck.

The depot gradually expanded and began to swallow up the former Down goods sidings. In 1967 work began on a new carriage shed capable of accommodating 36 vehicles along with reception sidings holding 60, and stabling and departure sidings to take 200. The new facilities were to replace the existing Neville Hill carriage shed on the Up side along with facilities at Copley Hill and Bradford. A three-year programme of further modernisation completed in 1978 saw the roundhouse converted into a straight maintenance shed for High Speed Trains as well as new cleaning and servicing sheds built for coaches and DMUs. The depot has seen further upgrades since then. And since the 1970s, Neville Hill has enjoyed an allocation of main line express passenger locomotives - direct successors to the A1s and A3s in the shape of the Class 43s - the HST power cars.

STEAM LOCOMOTIVES ALLOCATED TO 50B NEVILLE HILL JANUARY 1957

Fowler Class 3 2-6-2T: 40045/59; A3 Pacific: 60036 *Colombo*/60074 *Harvester*/60081 *Shotover*/60084 *Trigo*/60086 *Gainsborough*; B1 4-6-0: 61035 *Pronghorn*/61062/65/69/86/1216/18/61237 *Geoffrey H. Kitson*/61240 *Harry Hinchcliffe*/56/57/59; B16/1 4-6-0: 61411/12/13/14/15/25/27/28/29//31/32/42/46/47/70/71; D49 4-4-0: 62740 *The Bedale*/62742 *The Braes of Derwent*/62748 *The Southwold*/62749 *The Cottesmore*/62764 *The Garth*; Q6 0-8-0: 63348/436; J39 0-6-0: 64758/91/835/50/63/70/86/920/22/33/34/35/42/44; J25 0-6-0: 65648/50/54/83; G5 0-4-4T: 67262/74; J72 0-6-0T: 68672; A8 4-6-2T: 69881/5; WD 2-8-0: 90082/467/663. Total: 68

Classic 4-4-0s and coaling facilities old and new at Neville Hill.
Above: The modern mechanized coal plant towers over D21(NER Class R1) 4-4-0 LNER No. 1243 in May 1939. Built in June 1909, No. 1243 was withdrawn from service in June 1945. *Neville Stead collection*

Below: The unique D49/4 4-4-0 No. 2768 *The Morpeth* takes water by the old coal stage on 13th July 1947. No. 2768 had been rebuilt from a D49/2 in 1942 with inside cylinders of the pattern used on the Great Central D11 class. It was withdrawn in the early 1950s, well before the rest of the class. *G.H. Butland/Peter Rose collection*

Top: Class 04/3 2-8-0 No. 3835, one of the Railway Operating Division locomotives built to the Robinson Great Central design from 1917 and taken over by the LNER in 1924, sits outside Neville Hill's repair shop in around 1947. No. 3835 was a Tyne Dock engine at the time but was allocated to Hull Dairycoates by 1950. An ex-NER Class C7 Atlantic stands behind the O4. *Bob Lingwood/Peter Rose colln.*

Centre: Members of the Bradford Railway Circle pose with N13 0-6-2T No. 69117 during a visit to the shed on 28th September 1952. In 1950 Neville Hill had four of these ex-Hull & Barnsley Railway veterans for shunting and local trips. The other five survivors were all at Hull Springhead.

Bottom: Adding to the variety on 13th July 1947 was one of Neville Hill's five Gresley V1 2-6-2Ts, No. 7645, standing with a B16/1 4-6-0 by the famous water tower. *Both G.H. Butland/ Peter Rose collection*

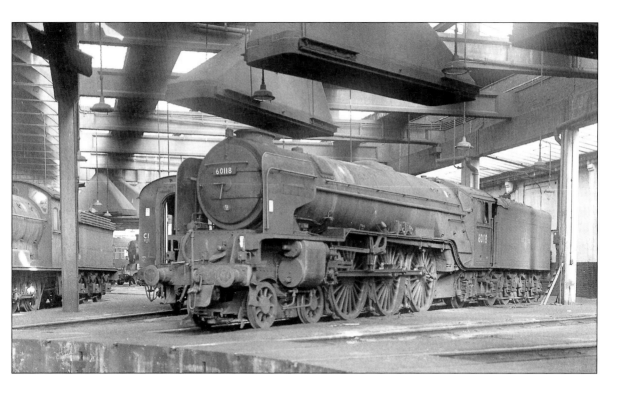

Above: Sitting inside the roundhouse at 16.43 on 18th September 1965 was A1 Pacific No. 60118 *Archibald Sturrock,* shorn of its name-plate and less than a month from withdrawal. On the left is a Q6 0-8-0 while in the background, between the encroaching DMU cars, is privately owned N7 0-6-2T No. 69621 which spent 14 years stored at Neville Hill. *Both pictures on this page by Robert Anderson*

Below: Since the end of steam, the roundhouse was used for housing a variety of vehicles including preserved steam locomotives. This was the scene on 9th July 1970 - looking remarkably similar to the one above except that A2 Pacific No. 532 *Blue Peter* shines a bit more than its A1 cousin! Behind it is A4 *Bittern* and on the right are the N7, K1 2-6-0 No. 62005 and K4 No. 3442 *The Great Marquess.*

Above: Neville Hill depot yard as it was on 28th April 1973 when a public open weekend was held. The DMU servicing shed is in the foreground and at the Leeds end Preserved LNER A4 Pacific No. 4498 *Sir Nigel Gresley* is engaged in giving rides up and down the yard with a single coach. Also at the far end is a "Peak" Type 4 diesel and on the left the expanse of carriage sidings. *Robert Anderson*

LOCOMOTIVES ALLOCATED TO NEVILLE HILL 1ST MAY 1965

Fairburn Class 4 2-6-4T: 42184/96/689/99; Ivatt Class 4 2-6-0: 43054/75; A1 4-6-2: 60118 *Archibald Sturrock*/ 60131 *Osprey*/ 60134 *Foxhunter*/60154 *Bon Accord*; K1 2-6-0: 62007; Q6 0-8-0: 63344/417/20/26; BR/Gardner 204hp 0-6-0: D2150; Drewry 204p 0-6-0: D2242/3/4/6/7; 350hp 0-6-0: D3375/657. Total: 23

Neville Hill depot had four local freight trip workings listed in the York District Local Freight & Mineral Trains book issued on 19th September 1955 besides No. 3 trip mentioned on page 51 and those booked in the working timetable. These were: **NH2,** a class K pick-up which left Neville Hill sidings at 5.25am(the loco leaving the shed at 5.5am) ran untimed non-stop to Tadcaster via Church Fenton and then shunted intermediate stations via Thorp Arch, Wetherby and back to Neville Hill via Scholes; **NH4,** a class H mineral train which left Neville Hill at 1.38pm(loco off shed at 1.23) and ran untimed to Stourton and back before running to Garforth and Peckfield Colliery and back; **NH5,** an untimed class H mineral train booked to leave Neville Hill at 4.25am(loco off shed at 4.10) which ran Kippax-Bowers-Castleford-Bowers-Castleford-Normanton-Castleford-Fryston Colliery-Wheldale Colliery-Allerton By-water Colliery-Kippax-Allerton Bywater and/or Bowers-Garforth-Neville Hill; and **NH6**, also a class H mineral train which left Neville Hill at 1.40pm(loco off shed at 1.25) for Peckfield and back, then to Normanton and back via Garforth, Allerton Bywater, Castleford, Bowers and Kippax.

In late 1955 Neville Hill was supplying shunting engines for eight pilot duties. **Marsh Lane No. 2** pilot(No.1 was suspended) worked 4.45am-4pm Mon-Sat inc. "attaches load at Neville Hill due Marsh Lane 4.45am. Shunts as required and conveys load to Neville Hill if necessary on completion." **Neville Hill No.1** worked 6am Mon-6am Sun: marshalling traffic in "Down yard, goods sections." **Neville Hill No.2** worked 6am Mon-6am Sun "marshalling traffic in Down yard mineral section and transferring wagons between Up and Down yards." **Neville Hill No.3** worked 6am Mon-6pm Sun "marshalling traffic in Up yard goods section." **Neville Hill No.4** worked 6am to 10pm each weekday "marshalling traffic in Up yard mineral section." **Neville Hill carriage sidings No. 1** shunted the carriage sidings as required; **Wellington Street No. 1** shunted Wellington Street North goods depot as required; and the **Hunslet** pilot shunted Hunslet East 5.20am-12 noon/1.20pm-4.30pm/5.10pm-7.20pm each weekday "shunting NER yard. Trip to exchange sidings and ER yard as necessary."

Above: One of the last surviving ex-Hull & Barnsley Railway 0-6-2Ts of LNER and BR Class N13, No. 69114, was a Neville Hill yard pilot on 6th July 1954. *Neville Stead collection*

Below: Fifteen years later and we are seeing just about the last steam action at Neville Hill Up yard as this Skipton fireman and his 9F 2-10-0 No. 92160 prepare to leave with the 20.15 empty tanks to Heysham on either the 10th, 11th or 12th June 1968. A Drewry 0-6-0 diesel shunter(Class 04) now has the pilot duty. *Peter Rose*

Above: Healey Mills yard was in full swing by this time and Neville Hill Up yard was reduced to handling local traffic and carriage and wagon stabling. This was the east end on 4th September 1967 where, as can be seen, one other function was to interchange with the National Coal Board line from Waterloo Main Colliery. An Austerity 0-6-0ST has just arrived at the exchange sidings with a load from the colliery as a BR/Sulzer Class 25 marshals the stock of a parcels train. *Robert Anderson*

Below: Obviously a late harvest in 1963 - a pair of Austerity 0-6-0STs top and tail a train of fulls from Waterloo Main as it climbs up to Neville Hill at mid-day on 9th October. The Presflo wagon next to the nearest engine makes a curious addition to the consist. The leading engine is *Jess* and the banker NCB3. Steam worked on the Waterloo Colliery system until November 1968. *Brian Myland*

Above: One of the Liverpool Bank Hall Jubilees so associated with the L&Y Calder Valley main line, No. 45698 *Mars*, and Stanier Class 5 No. 44891 double-head the Newcastle-Manchester Red Bank empty news vans past Neville Hill East on 19th April 1960. Neville Hill East signal box, 1008 yards from Neville Hill West, is on the right along with the entrance roads to the Up yard while one of the newly completed diesel depot buildings is on the left. Neville Hill East and West boxes were abolished per the 4-weekly notice issued on 15th February 1969 and the line to Peckfield brought under Leeds power box. *John Beaumont/Robert Anderson archive*

Below: On 19th September 1965, A4 No. 60004 *William Whitelaw* of Aberdeen Ferryhill shed, worked a RCTS railtour from Leeds to the Blyth & Tyne lines in Northumberland. Here, the Pacific brings the empty coaches off the old Neville Hill carriage depot at 08.50 and heads for City station to greet its assembled admirers. *Robert Anderson*

Above: Just east of Neville Hill was the timber halt at Osmondthorpe, seen here with A3 Pacific No. 60040 *Cameronian* of Darlington shed heading a Newcastle to Liverpool relief at 1.19pm on 6th June 1960. With Holbeck having a Royal Scot called *Cameronian* on its books, what were the odds of two engines with the same name but of different classes appearing in Leeds City at the same time? Osmondthorpe catered for passengers only and in summer 1957 was served by 15 weekday trains to Leeds, three to Hull, two to Selby, two to Harrogate via Wetherby and one each to Church Fenton, Tadcaster via Church Fenton, and York plus a Saturday Only train each to Garforth and Scholes. The halt closed on 7th March 1960 and since then all sign of it has disappeared(though a modernized foot-bridge marks the site) and the Slow lines(re-classified Goods lines in the 1960s) removed. *Both Robert Anderson*

Below: Cross Gates, 4.5 miles east of Leeds City. Neville Hill A3 No. 60074 *Harvester* speeds the Glasgow-bound North Briton effort-lessly past the well-tended platforms at 9.24am on 24th June 1961 as the goods shed and yard crane loom above on the right. Con-nected to the main line by a short branch which passed over the Wetherby line to a junction at Barnbow ordnance factory sidings, the goods yard was listed in the 1956 Stations Handbook as having a 1.5 ton crane and being equipped to handle only general goods and livestock. It closed on 1st June 1964. *Robert Anderson*

Above: How the scene was changing at Cross Gates, even in the 1960s. On 18th March 1967, one of Neville Hill's Birmingham RC&W Class 104 DMUs, working the 12.20 Leeds-Hull local, is held in the platform to allow passage of Britannia Pacific No. 70025 *Western Star,* seen bearing down on it with the 1X33 Barrow to Hull Rugby League special which had been delayed 17 minutes at Leeds City. The goods shed has gone and new development is taking its place. Since then the platform canopies have been removed and by 1968 the Fast lines through the centre had been lifted and the signal box, which was behind the photographer, abolished. *Robert Anderson* Proposals put forward in the early 1990s involved reopening the Wetherby line as a single track to Stanks Park and Ride on the A64 York road with an intermediate station at Scholes, reinstatement of four lines to Neville Hill, a new island platform in the centre at Cross Gates and a new three-platform station at Halton Dial, near the site of Osmondthorpe.

Below: Garforth station, 7.25 miles east of Leeds City, retains much of its original character in 2009, not least the NER pattern footbridge which will no doubt disappear should the line to York be electrified as is proposed. Brush Type 4 No. 47827 roars through with the 07.55 Birmingham-York on 6th March 1997. *Stephen Chapman*

Above: A beautiful portrait of a beautiful engine - and how pleasing to see an original B16 in such spotless condition. Neville Hill's No. 61425 rounds the curve from Leeds City to Whitehall Junction with a late 1950s stopping train to Ripon.
J.W. Haigh/Neville Stead collection

Below: One of the old NER roundhouses at Holbeck, as seen from the approach to Leeds Central in the 1950s, with more shed buildings on the extreme right. The shed closed in 1904 when the NER opened Neville Hill but as can be seen it was still in rail-served use by engineers Thos. Marshall & Son Ltd. at this time. All the main buildings but for a third roundhouse added by the NER in 1873 still stand in 2009 and can be viewed at close quarters. The lines in the foreground lead from Geldard Junction to Leeds Central and Wellington Street goods yard. *Ken Hoole/Neville Stead collection*

BR Goods depots and sidings in Leeds 1956

Armley Bridge(Mid./NE)

Armley Road Coal Depots(NE)

Cardigan Road(NE)

Copley Hill(LNW) - *general goods and livestock.*

Hunslet Balm Road(Mid.)

Hunslet East(GN & NE)

Hunslet Lane(Mid.)

Hunslet Pepper Rd.(GN) - *4-ton crane; general goods.*

Leeds Bonded Stores(LNW/L&Y)

Leeds Central (GN/LNW/L&Y/NE) - *with 1-ton crane; furniture vans, carriages, motor cars, portable engines, machines on wheels, livestock, horse boxes and prize cattle vans, and carriages and motor cars by passenger or parcels train.*

Leeds City(Mid.) - *horse boxes,prize cattle vans, carriages and motor cars by passenger or parcels train.*

Leeds City(LNW/NE) - *furniture vans, carriages, motor cars, portable engines, machines on wheels, horse boxes, prize cattle vans and carriages and motor cars by passenger or parcels train.*

Marsh Lane(NE) - *5 ton crane; livestock and furniture vans, carriages, motor cars, portable engines and machines on wheels.*

Wellington St. North(GN) - *6 ton crane; all classes of freight.*

Wellington St. North(NE)

Wellington St. South(LNW/L&Y) - *10 ton crane; general goods, livestock, furniture vans, carriages, motor cars, portable engines and machines on wheels.*

West Yorkshire Sidings(GN) - *coal, mineral and side to side wagonload traffic only.*

Whitehall Road(LNW/L&Y) - *20 ton crane; general goods, furniture vans, carriages, motor cars, portable engines and machines on wheels.*

Above: Viewed from near Leeds Central "B' signal box, Neville Hill J77 0-6-0T No. 68395 shunts the NE goods depot at Wellington Street North in the mid-1950s. The goods shed is visible in the background while a loading dock and coal drops are on the left. A Copley Hill J50 is shunting the GN side.

This depot was listed in the 1956 Stations Handbook as equipped with maximum cranage capacity of 6 tons and able to deal with general goods, livestock, furniture vans, carriages, motor cars, portable engines and machines on wheels. *John Beaumont*

Below: In 2003/4 morning peak Knaresborough-Leeds and evening peak return trains were loco-worked by train operator Arriva using English Electric Type 3(Class 37) locomotives hired from freight operator EWS, much to the delight of the gricing fraternity. In between these, they worked a service to Carlisle and back. The final run was on 24th September when 37408 *Loch Rannoch* was caught heading the 17.43 to Knaresborough past Wortley Junction. No. 37411 was on the rear. *Stephen Chapman*

Above: On the Leeds Northern line to Harrogate, A4 No. 60004 *William Whitelaw* tackles the bank up from Wortley Junction to Head-ingley with customary aplomb as it heads the RCTS Blyth & Tyne railtour on 19th September 1965. It is passing Cardigan Road goods yard which the 1956 Handbook of Stations listed as equipped with a 5-ton crane and equipped to handle only coal, mineral and "side to side" wagonload traffic, the coal drops just visible on the left. In winter 1959/60 Cardigan Road was served by the 6.10am Neville Hill-Otley class K pick-up which was booked to shunt there from 7 to 7.45am, and a class K trip booked to arrive from Neville Hill at 10.50am, returning at 11.16 with the working timetable instruction "clears empties from Cardigan Road. Starts from Horsforth or Headingley as required." Cardigan Road yard remained in use for coal until 4th September 1972 when rail deliveries ended.

Below: Preserved K4 2-6-0 No. 3442 *The Great Marquess* lollops up past the northern end of Cardigan Road yard while en-route to Dar-lington via Harrogate with the Leeds portion of an Ian Allan railtour at 11.49 on 3rd October 1964. *Both Robert Anderson*

Above: Looking over the west end of Leeds City from the Aire Street railway offices at 13.43 on 30th July 1965. In the foreground are the River Aire, Leeds City North station, carriage sidings and Wellington signal box while the departing 11.00 Liverpool-Newcastle via Harrogate passing Leeds City West signal box is hauled by A1 Pacific No. 60134 *Foxhunter,* deputising for defective Type 4 diesel No. D245 which had needed assistance to Leeds from the Manchester Exchange station pilot, a Standard Class 5. *Robert Anderson*

Below: Dramatic departures with "two on the front" were a feature of Trans-Pennine expresses in steam days. Farnley Junction's 2P 4-4-0 No. 40581 pilots Liverpool Edge Hill rebuilt Patriot 4-6-0 No. 45534 *E. Tootal Broadhurst* out of Leeds City South at the head of a mid-1950s Liverpool express. Leeds New Station signal box was situated within the station on the right. *J.W. Haigh/N. Stead colln.*

Above: At 15.25 on 1st March 1967, one of the purpose-built Trans-Pennine Inter-City DMUs - displaying a headcode which says it should be coming the other way - passes "Black Five" 4-6-0 No. 45219 as it approaches Whitehall Junction on its journey from Hull to Liverpool Lime Street. No. 45219, which was towing sister locos 44726 and 45012 to their fate at Draper's scrapyard in Hull, waits helplessly while 44726's derailed tender on the extreme left is reunited with the track(see page 42.) *Robert Anderson*

Below: Away from their native haunt, some of the ex-Lancashire & Yorkshire Railway "Radial" 2-4-2 tanks dating from 1889 were to be found on Midland lines local services to Leeds until the mid-1950s. No. 50686, one of those rebuilt from 1910 onwards with a Belpaire firebox and allocated to Bradford Manningham, passes Whitehall Junction, probably en-route to Ilkley.
Neville Stead collection

Above: Royal Scot No. 46113 *Cameronian* gets the Thames-Clyde moving out of Leeds City North in the mid-1950s.
J.W. Haigh/Neville Stead collection

Below: The exploits of 9F 2-10-0s on express passenger trains have entered the annals of railway folklore. Overseen by Leeds City Wellington signal box at 11.50am on 12th August 1961, No. 92128 of 15C Leicester, moves the stock of the 12 noon express to Birmingham, which it then worked. *Robert Anderson*

Right: Royston-based Stanier Class 3 2-6-2T No. 40193 heads the 8.25am all stations to Sheffield Midland out of Leeds City North platform 4 on Friday 3rd November 1961. *Peter Rose*

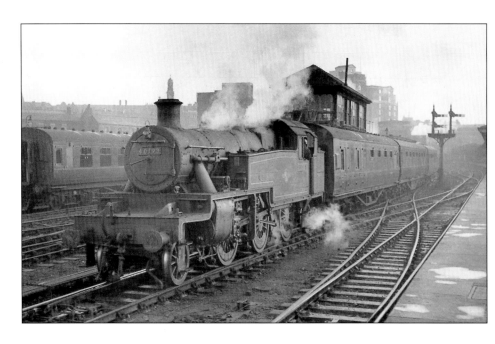

On 21st January 1963, Standard Class 5 4-6-0 No. 73060 of Glasgow Polmadie was on the 8.36pm Leeds to Hellifield slow.

Curios at Leeds City.

Left: For a time some ex-Caledonian Railway 2P 0-4-4 tanks were drafted into the area. On 16th August 1947 LMS No. 15227, one of the Pickersgill variant introduced in 1915, was found attached to a 6-wheel milk tank. *D. Butterfield/Neville Stead collection*

Bottom: These cut down goods vans, including a cattle truck, were in the sidings at Leeds Parcels Concentration Depot(formerly Leeds City North) on 19th March 1982. They were previously seen in the sidings at Horsforth and can be assumed to be part of the train used for maintenance of Bramhope Tunnel on the Harrogate line.

The former City of Leeds Electric Lighting Co. generating station, opened in 1902, is in the background. It has since been demolished, its place taken by modern "toy-town" apartments of the sort which now pen the station in on both sides. *S. Chapman*

On 5th January 1966, Edinburgh St. Margarets V2 2-6-2 No. 60824 worked the Thames-Clyde Express north from Leeds City.

SHORT MEMORIES

21.3.63: "Peak" No. D192 fails on the outskirts of Leeds with the 9.45am Newcastle-Liverpool and is rescued by Neville Hill A3 60086 *Gainsborough.*

May 1963: Brush Type 4s (Class 47s) make their debut on Leeds-King's Cross services. Only one steam diagram into Central remains - the 4am ex-London and the Up White Rose.

16.6.63: The 3.10pm King's Cross-Leeds & Bradford is the last booked steam passenger train from King's Cross. It is worked as far as Doncaster by A4 60008 *Dwight D. Eisenhower.*

12.1.65: The Thames-Clyde is among Midland expresses diverted to Central because of reconstruction at City station.

Above: Fowler 2-6-4T No. 42408 makes a rousing start from Leeds City North with the 6.42am Birmingham-Bradford at 10.38am on 17th February 1962.

Left: The 4F 0-6-0s were frequent performers on Midland line stopping passenger trains from Leeds. On 5th June 1960 Nottingham's No. 44578 pulls out of what was destined to become platform W(platform 1 since 2002) with the Sundays Only 1.50pm Bradford Forster Square-Derby semi-fast which it took over at Leeds. This train was formerly the preserve of a Compound 4-4-0 but after they were withdrawn, anything worked it. An Ivatt Class 2 2-6-0 stands on the right.
Both Robert Anderson

Left: The impressive Queens Hotel, completed by the LMS in 1938, dominates the right background with Aire Street offices on the left, as B1 No. 61194 awaits departure on the 11.11am Sheffield parcels on 30th July 1963. The 1938 parcels platform is on the left with the parcels office behind it. By the 1980s this part of the station was a car park.

Below: On 19th September 1966 Jubilee No. 45593 *Kolhapur* was spruced up and put on the 14.54 parcels to Wavertree specially for the BBC's Railway Roundabout TV programme. Leeds City North had been purely a parcels depot since June. *Both Robert Anderson*

Right: Transition at Leeds. Privatisation of BR inhibited funding of new trains for the Ilkley/Skipton electrification so refurbished old London suburban Class 308 units had to be used until new Class 333s entered service on 23rd January 2001. Viewed from newly opened platform W in 1998, a Class 308 waits in platform 1 of the 1960s station.

Above: Engineering work was doubtless the reason why the Harrogate Sunday Pullman was using City station on 21st October 1962(as was often the case in winter) with the Bradford portion going to Forster Square. One of Neville Hill's five ex-Whitby Standard Class 4 2-6-4 tanks is seen in City North's platform 6(today's platform 1) with the Harrogate train. Platform 6 and platform 5(left) were used for mail traffic until 1997. *D. Butterfield/Neville Stead collection*

Below: One of Holbeck's Stanier Class 5 4-6-0s modified with Caprotti valve gear, Timken roller bearings and a double chimney, brings the 7.42am Bradford Forster Square-Bristol into Leeds City South at 8.3am on 11th June 1962, just 21 minutes after leaving Bradford and with a stop at Shipley. *Robert Anderson*

Above: On the same occasion as on page 70, *Kolhapur* had to draw its train out of the parcels depot and then set back across the entire layout at Leeds City west end in order to access the Viaduct line for its run to Liverpool, the train's normal route via Copley Hill Goods being closed for relaying.

The two "Peaks" on the right are in the Motive Power Area, at that time including a turntable which had been removed by May 1967. The motive power sidings were abandoned by 1986. *Robert Anderson*

Below: Photographed by Holbeck fireman Roy Wood from the cab of his engine as it waited in the motive power area, Black Five No. 45219 makes a rousing start from the modern Leeds City with a Blackpool train on 22nd July 1967. A green Brush Type 4(Class 47) loiters at the end of the new platform 5, perhaps intending to work a King's Cross train. *Roy Wood/Peter Rose collection*

Above: Summer 1955, before DMUs took over and there was still a wondrous variety of vintage motive power and rolling stock to behold. Here, one of the Worsdell NER D20 4-4-0s built from 1899, No. 62372, arrives at Leeds City with a service from the Harrogate direction. *Neville Stead collection*

Below: On 29th February 1964 four football specials worked by North East-based A3s ran from Newcastle and Sunderland to Manchester, three via Horsforth and one via either York or Wetherby. One of those which came via Horsforth, reporting number 1X38, arrives behind No. 60070 *Gladiateur*, then allocated to Gateshead but also having spells at Holbeck and Neville Hill. Train 1X41 arrived behind 60051 *Blink Bonny* and 1X42 behind 60080 *Dick Turpin*, and IX45 which entered Leeds from the east, behind 60040 *Cameronian*. Train 1X38 was worked forward by Jubilee No. 45581 *Bihar and Orissa*. *John Beaumont/Robert Anderson archive*

Above: A lone airman waits despondently for his return to camp at 10.30am on 25th May 1963 as Black Five No. 45193 simmers with satisfaction at another job done, having arrived at platform 10 with the 7.57am from Carnforth. Beyond are platforms 7, 8 and 9 and the sidings that separated the South and North platforms until the 1999-2002 reconstruction when the space was filled with new platforms. The Leeds Electric Lighting Co. generating station towers over the North side platforms 5 and 6 canopy. *Robert Anderson*

Centre: The world's fastest steam loco, LNER A4 No. 4468 *Mallard*, was a regular at Central station in steam days. On this occasion, after restoration to working order in 1930s condition by the National Railway Museum to celebrate the 50th anniversary of her record run, she is at City station with a York-Carlisle special on 16th July 1988.

Left: From 1990, following East Coast electrification, three Class 307 electric trains previously carrying London commuters, were used on the Leeds-Doncaster local service until more modern Class 321s took over. *Stephen Chapman*

Above: This unusual view from the station roof shows 9F 2-10-0 No. 92154 sandwiched between "Peak" Type 4 No. D35 and an English Electric Type 3(Class 37) as it waits the road on the goods lines on the station's south flank with the 10.25 Hunslet East-Stanlow empty tanks on 31st May 1967. The Leeds-Liverpool canal wharf adds interest to the background. *Robert Anderson*
These goods lines were abandoned at the start of the winter 1999 timetable so that the present platforms 16 and 17 could be built, the 9F being on what is now the platform 17 bay. The canal wharf is now hidden by new tower blocks.

Left: Mail traffic was once an everyday feature of most stations but nowadays what little remains on the railway uses dedicated mail terminals. On 7th April 1967, flat barrows and BRUTE trolleys clutter the platform as Fairburn 2-6-4T No. 42085 waits for mail to be unloaded from the 13.50 St. Pancras-Bradford before taking the train on the last leg of its journey. Class 5 No. 44943 and 9F 92093 approach with the Heysham-Hunslet East tanks. *Robert Anderson*

Above: The Victorian triple arch trainshed roof of Leeds City South could never be admired for its architectural merit, unlike its near neighbour at York, but at least it still had a solid look about it on 9th July 1961 when it hosted a rare visitor in the form of Coronation Pacific No. 46247 *City of Liverpool* which was about to work a RCTS special to Carlisle. How different the scene would look in two years time. *Neville Stead collection*

Below: Another RCTS railtour, this time in June 1963 with Gateshead A4 No. 60023 *Golden Eagle* awaiting departure from what would become the new platform 12.
Jack Wild/Stephen Chapman archive

SHORT MEMORIES

4.9.65: A1 No. 60124 *Kenilworth* arrives at Leeds with a railtour from Birmingham after the booked A4, 60004 *William Whitelaw* fails.

27.3.66: Britannia 70005 *John Milton* noted minus nameplates on the line behind Farnley shed with Jubilee 45562 *Alberta*.

May 1966: Multiple aspect signalling installed from Cross Gates to Peckfield and the track rationalized.

1.3.67: 350hp diesel shunter D3658 is the tool van which turns up at Whitehall Jn. to rerail Black Five 44726's derailed tender - its cab, running plate and steps are crammed with men, jacks and packing.

10.8.68: Class 52 No. D1016 *Western Gladiator* is alleged to have passed through Leeds on northbound nuclear flasks.

October 1968: Leeds power signal box control area extended to Garforth

Above: The Harrogate Sunday Pullman at Leeds City again - this time at the South side. A1 No. 60156 *Great Central* brings the train from King's Cross past the imposing Leeds City West signal box on 1st October 1961. The Harrogate portion was worked forward via Wetherby by BR Standard 2-6-4T No. 80120 and the Bradford portion to Forster Square by Ivatt Class 4 2-6-0 No. 43117. *Roy Wood/Peter Rose collection*

Below: The new roof is going up but the old station's footbridge still stands alone as Class 5 4-6-0 No. 45196 waits to leave with the 10.47am to Morecambe and Carnforth at 10.40 on 16th November 1963. *Robert Anderson*

Above: This well composed vintage scene at the station's west end on 16th June 1958 shows ex-NER G5 0-4-4T No. 67325 beneath the train-shed extension removed in 1960/61. The G5 displays headlamps which suggest it has just brought empty coaches from Neville Hill.
Neville Stead collection

Centre: Hardly a stunning picture taken with a Brownie 44A camera but worthy of inclusion for its rarity. On a raw 15th January 1972 Leeds United were at home to Bristol Rovers in the third round of the FA Cup, beating them 4-1. This Western Region "Blue Pullman" set, which normally worked only between Paddington, Bristol and South Wales, brought the Bristol team, club officials and, no doubt, selected supporters. *Stephen Chapman*
On 9th March 1968 two Blue Pullman sets coupled together formed a football special from Bristol.

Left: When the nightmare that was - and in 2009 still is - the Pacer 4-wheeled railbuses began: the Class 140 prototype about to work the 12.50 to Marsden on 9th June 1981. During a demonstration run to Ilkley it was criticized for its rough ride and squealing on curves.

Above: The clash of eras is apparent in this scene showing the new 1960s City station still with NER-pattern water crane and Fairburn 2-6-4T No. 42699 removing empty coaches at 12.35 on 27th August 1965. Despite its number, 42699 - notably in unlined black livery - was one of the oldest Fairburns, being in the first batch built at Derby in 1945 and transferred from Dumfries to Neville Hill in 1963.

Below: The Leeds City which we probably remember best. On a damp and dismal 10th September 1977, preserved LNER A4 No. 4498 *Sir Nigel Gresley* waits in one of the bay sidings between platforms 2 and 3 before taking a special to York via Harrogate, as one of its successors, an unidentified Deltic, makes ready in platform 5 for its run to King's Cross. *Both Robert Anderson*

Above: A reminder of the variety which could once be seen at Leeds. In the bay platform area at 18.40 on 2nd June 1967, were, from left: A Birmingham RC&W "Calder Valley" DMU(Class 110) in platform 2, one of the last active Stanier Class 4 2-6-4Ts No. 42616, A BR/Gardner 204hp 0-6-0 diesel shunter(Class 03,) and in platform 3 a Derby Works(Class 114) DMU forming a service to Sheffield. *Robert Anderson. Picture Below: John Beaumont/Robert Anderson archive*

Below: The skeletal remains of the old trainshed stand like an ancient ruin as Doncaster V2 2-6-2 No. 60872, formerly *The King's Own Yorkshire Light Infantry,* restarts the 8.30am Manchester Victoria-Scarborough on 13th July 1963.

Above: A month earlier than the previous picture and demolition hasn't quite progressed as far. Manchester Newton Heath-allocated Jubilee No. 45654 *Hood* arrives at platform 11 with 1N75, the 9am Manchester Exchange-Filey Holiday Camp at 10.30 on 15th June 1963. Note the workmen on the roof - well before the age of Health and Safety law! *Robert Anderson*

Below: Beneath the lofty arcading of City South station's interior in February 1962, Patriot 4-6-0 No. 45507 *Royal Tank Corps* of 24J Lancaster after working in from Morecambe. *Peter Rose*

Above: In many British cities at one time, walking out of the station did not mean an end to rail transport. The gent with the pipe, suit (Burton's no doubt) and trilby cuts a dash as he crosses Briggate past Horsfall tramcar No.180 in 1959. *Jack Wild/Stephen Chapman archive*

Left: History is made as electrification arrives. Crewe-built Class 91 No. 91003 "tender first" in platform 5 with a test train formed of Mk1 coaches on 23rd September 1988. *Stephen Chapman*

Right: Dealing with over 800 trains a day was a demanding task for Leeds power box signalmen, especially in later years when the infrastructure was clapped out. The 1960s power box, seen here in the early 1990s, was commissioned between 18.00 on Saturday 29th April and 00.01 on Monday 1st May 1967, and was situated in the station office block. Since the turn of the 20th century, operations have been controlled from the signalling centre in York. *Eddie Toal*

Above: The 1960s station's interior is shown to good effect as Brush Type 4 No. 47615 arrives at platform 6 with the 10.40 to Carlisle in January 1988. *Stephen Chapman*

Below: How the same spot looked on 14th March 2001 when the reconstruction was at its height and platform 6 had already been renumbered platform 9. The 1960s trainshed roof remains in situ but the new roof is being built above it. *Stephen Chapman*

Above: The Victorian station roof looked quite different at the east end, being composed of a ramshackle selection of different styles. J39 0-6-0 No. 64934 departs with the 11.52am races special, one of several, to Wetherby on Easter Monday 23rd April 1962. *Peter Rose*

Below: This picture shows just how low the 1960s roof was and how dark the interior, but how much neater it was. One of Neville Hill's A1s, No. 60118 *Archibald Sturrock,* waits to take over the 09.05 Liverpool-Newcastle from Jubilee No. 45655 *Keith* on Sunday 11th October 1964. The train was 70 minutes late owing to engineering work and the failure of its booked diesel. *Robert Anderson*

Upon commissioning of the new Leeds City power box on 29th April-1st May 1967, the following signal boxes were closed: Leeds City East, Leeds City West, Leeds City Junction, Whitehall Junction, Wortley North, Wortley Junction, Leeds Central A, Leeds Central B, Holbeck Junction, Wortley South. Geldard Junction was retained for "working trains between the Arrival and Departure spurs and Wellington Goods Yards."

The new signalling control area reached as far as interface boxes at Wortley West, Morley Low, Beeston Junction, Engine Shed Junction, Kirkstall, Headingley and Neville Hill West.

Details of the new arrangements were set out in a Supplementary Programme of Signalling Arrangements effective from 29th April 1967 issued by British Rail Eastern(NE) Region.

Over the following years, the power box control area was progressively extended to meet fringe boxes at Methley, Batley, Doncaster, Bradford Mill Lane, Apperley Junction, Horsforth and Peckfield. At its ultimate, it also controlled all the way to Ilkley, Bradford Forster Square and Hellifield.

Above: The Victorian structure has finally gone and work has just begun on erecting the new station. A Trans-Pennine(Class 124) diesel set displaying a bizzarly inaccurate head-code, has just arrived as preserved LNER K4 2-6-0 No. 3442 *The Great Marquess* - almost as much a familiar sight here in the 1960s as the Trans-Pennines, waits to take on a special working on 25th April 1963. *Jack Wild/Stephen Chapman archive*

Below: Locomen with years of experience etched across their faces hold a conference at 12.25 on 9th June 1967. The crew of Fairburn 2-6-4T No. 42066 were adamant that they were pushing BR/Sulzer(Class 24) Type 2 diesel No. D5100 as well as pulling the train, the 11.55 Bradford Exchange to King's Cross. *Robert Anderson*

Above: For those of us who were kids in the 1960s, Lyons Maid Zoom ice lollies were as much a part of summer as the steam engines that inspired us. The two combined when Lyons Maid ran excursions for competition winners and one of the Lyons Maid Zoom specials is seen here entering Leeds City at 5.34pm on 6th September 1964 while returning from York to Liverpool. Again, *Great Marquess* is in action, piloting "Black Five" 4-6-0 No. 44767 - the only one with Stephenson link motion. *Robert Anderson*

Below: The thumping roar of Maybach engines in the Class 52 Westerns was normally confined to the Western Region but on 20th January 1977, with the class on the verge of extinction on BR, No. 1013 *Western Ranger* made it all the way to Leeds with the 07.30 from Swansea. The story goes that the booked loco had failed so 1013 was substituted to work as far as Birmingham but on arrival there, no steam heat-fitted loco was available so 1013's Gloucester driver agreed to work the loco through to Leeds with conductors providing route knowledge. After refuelling at Neville Hill, 1013 returned to the Western Region on the 14.43 to Plymouth. *Robert Anderson*

CENTRAL & THE GREAT NORTHERN

Above: Three miles out from Leeds Central the branches to Tingley and Hunslet East left the Doncaster line at Beeston Junction where Copley Hill A1 No. 60117 *Bois Roussel* is seen accelerating south with the Queen of Scots on 9th May 1959. The Hunslet East branch is hidden by the train while the Tingley lines leave ahead of it to form a flying junction. *P.B. Booth/Neville Stead collection*

Below: Along the Hunslet East branch was Parkside Junction where there were exchange sidings with the Middleton Railway to Broom Colliery and, until 1958, the Middleton fireclay works. These connections served a new Middleton Railway alignment which replaced the original 1758 line in 1881. On Saturday morning 22nd May 1965, WD 2-8-0 No. 90056 attaches the brake van to the loaded wagons it has just brought from the colliery before taking them to Ardsley as a B1 4-6-0 passes by with a trip to Hunslet East. *Brian Myland*

Middleton Broom Colliery. One locomotive only will be allowed to work in the sidings and on the colliery line. Before departure of a train to the colliery, the signalman will inform the NCB yard foreman who will arrange for protection of the level crossing near the colliery siding. Guards must obtain an assurance from the signalman that the yard foreman has been advised before allowing the train to proceed. The train must be drawn and convey a brake van in rear. Before the train leaves the colliery the guard must apply sufficient wagon brakes. *BR NE Region Sectional Appendix 1960*

Above: Having attached the brake van and run round its train at Hunslet East, WD 2-8-0 No. 90056 was photographed from Parkside Junction signal box while taking its train away to Ardsley Old Coal Yard. *Brian Myland*

The 1960 Sectional Appendix stated that the ground frame controlling access to Clayton & Son's Pepper Road siding between Parkside and Hunslet was secured by a lock, the key to which was kept in Parkside signal box. It instructed guards of trains attaching and detaching wagons at the siding to obtain the key from the box and return it there when work was complete. It continued: "A following train must not be allowed to leave Parkside in the direction of Hunslet until any train which has been at work at the siding has left and 'Train out of Section' has been received for it from Hunslet."

Below: The GN Hunslet East branch crossed the River Aire and the Aire & Calder Navigation on a huge triple-span girder bridge. Ardsley J94 Austerity 0-6-0ST No. 68011 rumbles a trip freight over the bridge and towards Hunslet East on 1st August 1961. After Hunslet East closed in 1966, the line was severed and buffer stops erected on the Hunslet side of the bridge to mark the end of the remaining branch from Neville Hill, the bridge eventually being removed. The section from Beeston Junction to Parkside remained in use until 1968 to serve Broom Colliery. *Peter Rose*

Hunslet East(GN) booked arrivals and departures.
Winter 1959/60 Working Timetable

am
4.23   4am class F from Ardsley
4.37   3.30amMX class J from
            Bradford Adolphus St.
5.30MX Engine & brake van to Ardsley
5.32MX 5.5 class H from Ardsley
6.0MX Engine & brake van to Ardsley
6.15   Class H to Ardsley
7.26   7.0 class H from Ardsley
9.5   Class J to Park Side Jn.
9.51   9.25 class H from Ardsley
10.40 Class H to Laisterdyke
11.10 11.0 class J from Park Side Jn.
pm
1.10SO 12.40 class H from Ardsley
1.15   Class K to Ardsley
1.45SO Class J to Batley East
3.25SX 3.15 class J from Park Side Jn.
4.45SX Class J to Ardsley
5.21SX 4.28 class K from Ardsley
            Shunts Park Side 4.42-5.1 and
            Pepper Road Siding 5.7-5.16
5.26SX Class H to Ardsley
7.33SX Class H to Ardsley
7.38SX 7.15 Engine & brake van from
                          Ardsley
8.30SX Class J to Laisterdyke
9.0SX   Class H to Ardsley

Fitton's Siding. Box wagons must not be shunted into, nor must locomotives enter the firm's building at the end of this siding.
NE Region Sectional Appendix 1960

Right: An extensive railway network ran from Waterloo Colliery to the NER main line at Neville Hill, coal depots and Hunslet East, and to this staithe for barges on the Navigation, disused by the time this photograph was taken from the Hunslet East line on 1st August 1961. Knostrop Waterworks fills the background.
Peter Rose

Apart from Knostrop Waterworks, other industrial concerns in Leeds with their own locomotives during the mid-1970s were: Kirkstall Power Station with a Hudswell Clarke 0-4-0 diesel; Skelton Grange Power Station with three Yorkshire Engine Co. 0-6-0 diesels and a Fowler 0-6-0 diesel; Miles Druce with their Barclay 0-4-0 diesel at Hunslet; and the Ministry of Defence ordnance factory at Cross Gates with Hibberd diesel 3918/59.

Above: One of the lesser-known railways in Leeds - until one of the above locomotives was restored by Channel Four TV's Salvage Squad - was the 1ft 11.5 inch system at Knostrop Waterworks.
These two armoured Motorail 4-wheeled Petrol locos, works Nos. 1369 and 1377 outside the neat loco shed on 13th July 1979, were built in 1918 for military service in the first world war which ended before they saw action. Also at Knostrop was a Ruston diesel built in 1960. The rail system was out of use by the 1980s. *Adrian Booth*

Left: A branch from Hunslet East yard to Knostrop Waterworks was abandoned long before this picture was taken on 1st August 1961, yet a GNR somersault signal was still guarding the former crossing with the line to the canal staithe. Some waterworks railway skips can just be discerned in front of the buildings in the right background. *Peter Rose*

Above: Crossing the intersection with the original LNW line to Huddersfield on 2nd March 1963 with the 4.10pm Leeds Central to Cleethorpes is Immingham-based Britannia Pacific No. 70035 *Rudyard Kipling*. Displaced by Brush Type 2 diesels on Cleethorpes-King's Cross services, the Britannias were put to work on the Leeds service. *Robert Anderson*

Below: A1 No. 60135 *Madge Wildfire* hauls the Up Yorkshire Pullman past Wortley South Junction at 10.50am on 11th November 1961. Copley Hill loco shed and a J6 0-6-0 are in the background. In the foreground, going off to the left is the curve to Wortley West Junction which provided a direct route between Bradford Exchange and the Doncaster line. It was closed in the early 1980s amid controversy because Bradford-London trains then had to make a time-consuming detour via Leeds. In 2009 only two electrified running lines remain at this spot yet some track survives on the Wortley curve, overgrown and disconnected from the Doncaster and Bradford lines. *Robert Anderson*

Above: On 15th June 1963, B1 4-6-0 No. 61016 *Inyala* passes its home depot at Copley Hill as it sets out from Leeds with the 9.55am Leeds Central to Great Yarmouth. *Robert Anderson*

Below: Deltic No. D9012 *Crepello* roars up to Copley Hill on 12th February 1963 with the 12.55pm Leeds Central to King's Cross, the first vehicle of which is a dynamometer car testing the efficiency of the Deltic's train heating boiler. *Robert Anderson*

Following the introduction of Deltics on 11th September 1961, the 7.45pm West Riding from King's Cross becomes the fastest timed train on BR and its overall journey time is cut by 44 minutes. The Up Yorkshire Pullman is 47 minutes quicker, the Up West Riding 45 minutes quicker, and the 5.29pm from Leeds is 55 minutes quicker.

Copley Hill(coded 37B in the Ardsley district of BR's Eastern Region until 1956 when it was transferred to the North Eastern Region and became 56C in the Wakefield district) was situated in the triangle formed by the Bradford Exchange and Doncaster lines and the Wortley Curve connecting the two. The former Great Northern depot for Leeds, it was almost entirely a passenger shed, providing engines for both express and local services on the former GN lines out of Leeds Central to Doncaster, King's Cross, Bradford Exchange and Castleford as well as engines for local pilot and empty coaching stock work. Main line goods engines were provided by Ardsley depot, situated between here and Wakefield Westgate. Its allocation was not always entirely ex-GN and LNER. In the 1960s it received a number of ex-LMS types, including 2-6-4 tank engines and even a brace of "Black Five" 4-6-0s, and for a short time in 1957 it was allocated four North Eastern G5 0-4-4 tanks.

When diesel multiple units took over most local services from the 1950s onwards followed by diesel locomotives on the London turns, none were allocated to Copley Hill and it remained entirely a steam depot. As such, its allocation steadily dwindled until 9th September 1964 when it became the second major locomotive depot in Leeds to close(the L&Y shed nextdoor having closed some 30 years before.) The shed was quickly demolished and the site cleared and ultimately redeveloped to become a steel stockholding warehouse which was not rail connected.

Above: The west end of Copley Hill shed at 5pm on 12th April 1963 with typical 56C motive power on display. From right are: Fowler 2-6-4T No. 42411, A1s 60133 *Pommern* and 60141 *Abbotsford*, B1 4-6-0 No. 61023 *Hirola* and A3 No. 60092 *Fairway*. The main line to Doncaster is on the right and the carriage shed on the left. The GN loco shed was rebuilt by BR in the 1950s. *Robert Anderson*

LOCOMOTIVES ALLOCATED TO 56C COPLEY HILL JANUARY 1957

A3 4-6-2: 60051 *Blink Bonny*/60052 *Prince Palatine*/60053 *Sansovino*/60058 *Blair Athol*; A1 4-6-2: 60117 *Bois Roussel*/60118 *Archibald Sturrock*/60120 *Kittiwake*/60130 *Kestrel*/60131 *Osprey*/60133 *Pommern*/60134 *Foxhunter*/60141 *Abbotsford*/60148 *Aboyeur;* V2 2-6-2: 60859/65/85/913; B1 4-6-0: 61129/1309/86/87/88; J6 0-6-0: 64173/276/77; J39 0-6-0: 64911; G5 0-4-4T: 67246/80/311/29; C13 4-4-2T: 67433/38; J50 0-6-0T: 68911/13/25/37/78/84/88; N1 0-6-2T: 69450/69. Total: 40.

LOCOMOTIVES ALLOCATED TO 56C COPLEY HILL SEPTEMBER 1964

Fairburn Class 4 2-6-4T: 42073; Stanier Class 4 2-6-4T: 42622; Ivatt Class 4 2-6-0: 43101/37; A1 4-6-2: 60117 *Bois Roussel*/60130 *Kestrel*/60133 *Pommern*/60148 *Aboyeur;* B1 4-6-0: 61031 *Reedbuck*/1382/85. Total: 11

Left: Fowler 2-6-4T No. 42411 at the front refuses to be humbled by its distinguished companions at the west end of Copley Hill shed on a dreary 13th April 1963. From front to back, they are: A1 No. 60141 *Abbotsford*, A4 No. 60026 *Miles Beevor* and A1 No. 60133 *Pommern*. The carriage shed is behind while St. Mary's church keeps watch. *Robert Anderson*

Above: J50 0-6-0T No. 68988 draws forward to the points at the west end of Copley Hill depot at 6.7pm on 12th April 1963 after bringing empty stock from Central station which it has just deposited immediately left of the carriage shed. Wortley East signal box can be seen standing aloof of the carriage shed while the coaling stage protrudes above the engine shed on the right. The sidings on the extreme left, towards the back, mark the site of the Lancashire & Yorkshire engine shed. *Robert Anderson*

Below: Unlike its neighbours at Holbeck, Neville Hill and Farnley Junction, Copley Hill, like Stourton, never received the benefit of a mechanical coaling plant. At 5.4pm on 12th April 1963 one of the aliens among the shed's allocation, Stanier Class 5 4-6-0 No. 44912 - still sporting the early BR totem on its tender - is replenished at the old ramped coal stage. Coal from wagons pushed up on to the ramp behind the stage, was transhipped into tubs and then tipped into the locomotive's tender. *Robert Anderson*

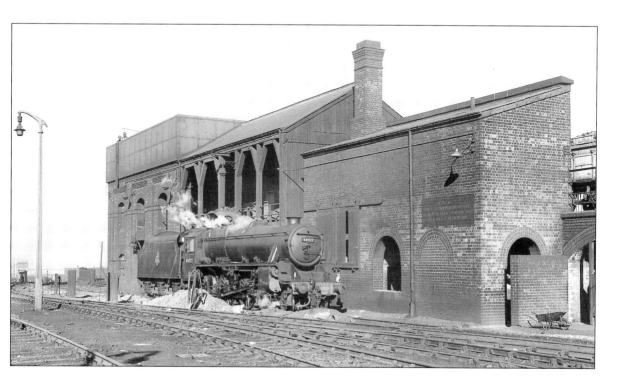

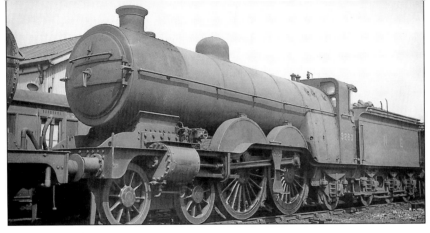

Left: Before the Pacifics, the GN Atlantics were prime power for London trains. Copley Hill's own LNER Class C1 No. 3280 stands in the shed yard on 11th July 1946. It was withdrawn before it could carry its new number, 2809.
Bob Lingwood/ Peter Rose colln.

Below: The layout at Copley Hill in 1921 showing the former Lancashire & Yorkshire Railway shed as well as the GN depot.
Not to scale

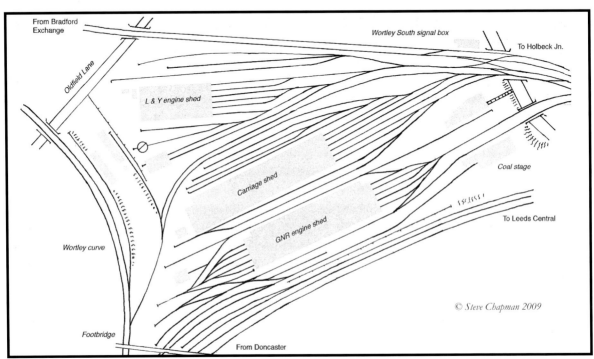

From Bradford Exchange

Wortley South signal box

To Holbeck Jn.

Oldfield Lane

L & Y engine shed

Coal stage

Carriage shed

To Leeds Central

GNR engine shed

Wortley curve

© Steve Chapman 2009

Footbridge

From Doncaster

Right: A J50 0-6-0T and J6 0-6-0 No. 64226 grace the west end of Copley Hill shed at 3.45pm on 17th February 1962. There looks to have once been a turntable bottom right but none is shown on the 1921 Ordnance Survey sheet. *Robert Anderson*

Above: It is 23rd March 1963 and there are only about three months to go before steam is eliminated from King's Cross trains. Even so, A4 No. 60010 *Dominion of Canada* confidently ascends the climb up to Copley Hill with the 12.55pm from Leeds. *Robert Anderson*

Below: With diesels having taken its top link work, A1 No. 60130 *Kestrel* manages to stay active by working the 10.10am Leeds-Doncaster stopping train in place of the usual DMU on Whit. Monday 18th May 1964. It is seen climbing past Holbeck Junction with the signal box, the line to Bradford Exchange and Wortley gas works on the left. *Robert Anderson*

Above: A fine overview of the western exit from Leeds with preserved A3 No. 4472 *Flying Scotsman* bringing the Epsom College Railway Society special of 17th April 1967, which it will work throughout to King's Cross, past Holbeck High Level station. On the right are the realigned LNW lines to Leeds City with points installed ready to make a connection at Holbeck Junction allowing GN line trains to reach City station. The original LNW line on the far right is now just a headshunt for Whitehall Road goods yard. *Robert Anderson* In summer 1957, Holbeck High Level was served by no less then 97 trains each weekday, with services to Bradford, Halifax, Manchester Victoria, Liverpool Exchange, Castleford via Stanley, Doncaster and King's Cross - including the Up West Riding at 7.54am

Below: Lest we forget the Great Central had an involvement in Leeds, being able to use the GN lines to reach Central station, its Robinson Class C13 4-4-2 tanks were among the local passenger fleet once allocated to Copley Hill. Push-pull version No. 67438 takes a local service away from Leeds Central, leaving "B" signal box in the background, in October 1954. *J.W. Haigh/Neville Stead collection.*

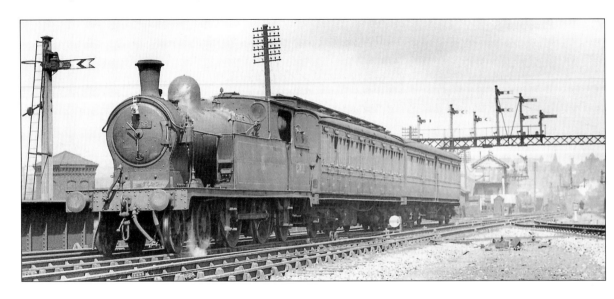

Above: The country's first diesel multiple units soon developed teething troubles and "foreign" engines had to be drafted in to substitute for them, including some Great Eastern N7 0-6-2Ts. In October 1954 the fireman of Low Moor-based BR Class 2 2-6-2T No. 84014, probably working the Leeds portion of an express to Liverpool Exchange via the L&Y, looks back on N7 No. 69695 as it propels a push-pull service towards Central station. No. 69695 was one of four N7s re-allocated to Copley Hill from elsewhere in the Eastern Region. *J.W. Haigh/N. Stead colln.*

Below: The view from "B" box towards Central station with J50 0-6-0T No. 68925 removing a single wagon to Copley Hill. The lines going off left lead into the LNW/L&Y Wellington Street High Level goods depot. Right of the guard's van visible through 68925's smoke haze is a wagon hoist tower used to move wagons into another goods shed on Whitehall Road. *Peter Rose*

Above: Leeds Central from "A" box on a grim November day in 1966. Copley Hill shed is history and Holbeck's Fairburn 2-6-4T No. 42699 is on pilot duty as a Deltic waits in the turntable siding and a Calder Valley DMU lurks deep inside. Christmas parcels stack up on the platform on the left. *Jack Wild/S. Chapman archive*

Below: More traditional power for empty stock, J6 0-6-0 No. 64203 brings London Midland Region coaches into the station at 12.43pm on 5th August 1961.
David Holmes

Working of LMS and LNER freight trains crossing at Leeds "B" box. The 1937 LMS Sectional Appendix stated that trains from Copley Hill to Armley Sidings[for Wellington Street North] must not exceed the equivilant of 26 ordinary wagons and 40 ton brake van or two 20 ton brake vans in length. The brake van had to be at the leading end when trains were being propelled from Copley Hill towards Leeds Central. One 20 ton brake van sufficed when trains did not exceed 12 wagons.Trains from Armley Sidings in clear weather must not exceed in length the equivilant of 27 ordinary wagons and one 20 ton brake van in the rear between 4.15am and 10.30pm on weekdays. Between 10.30pm and 4.15am, and 10.30pm Sat. and 4.15am Monday, the load could be made up to 40 ordinary wagons and one 20 ton brake van.

During fog or falling snow trains in either direction had to have an assisting engine at the rear but could be made up to 24 ordinary wagons, a brake van not being necessary, the guard riding on the rear engine.

Leeds Central. Consignments of more than three truck loads of slow vans cannot be dealt with at Leeds Central, and under no circumstances must the weight of any slow van exceed 50cwt.
LMS 1937 Central Division Sectional Appendix

Above: One of the two steam-powered hoists used to lower wagons from the Central station area to the low level goods depots, still standing after the rest had been cleared.
Stephen Chapman

Left: Leeds Central "A" signal box in November 1966.

Below: No one could ever accuse Central station of being ostentatious. This was its humble main entrance in November 1966. It's hardly a classic, but the cars and Rowntree's delivery van have to be. *Both Jack Wild/Stephen Chapman archive*

The pictures on these two pages show a selection of scenes which tell us more about the old Central station than its trains can.

Left: The concourse looking south.

Centre: The view towards the buffer stops during a quiet moment with the back of W.H. Smith's bookstall on the left and the buffet(regularly used by Jimmy Saville and actress Violet Carson, aka Ena Sharples) on the right. Posters include one advising arriving passengers to "switch to Inter-City."

Bottom: The station has come to life with the arrival at platform 2 of Deltic No. D9018 *Ballymoss* on an Inter-City train from King's Cross formed Mk1 coaches in BR's new standard blue and white livery.
All three pictures date from November 1966 and five months later this terminus, whose modest looks hide its importance, will have closed. On its last day, 30th April 1967, the last departure for London was at 17.50 and the last one to Harrogate at 18.10. *Jack Wild/Stephen Chapman archive*

On Central's last day, Yorkshire Evening Post reporter Ronald Wilkinson wrote: "Paint peels from the grimy woodwork and the rusty iron struts that support the roof. Dust lies thick on ledges, in corners, and on the eight benches bearing the inscription "Leeds Central." The odorous tiled icebox along one wall is the nadir in gentlemen's conveniences.

"Staring back at the dirty face of the clock, is a blank departures board on which has been posted a new timetable referring to the mammoth acquisitive City station."

Above: The concourse looking north, also in November 1966. The Christmas tree provides some cheer while a poster on Smith's bookstall proclaims the delights of the Meccano Magazine for two shillings(10P) with free Dinky Ford Zodiacs and another features President Kennedy, LP records are on the stands at 12 shillings apiece and The Venetian Affair is showing at The Odeon. *Jack Wild/Stephen Chapman archive*

Below: A scene which emphasizes the reality of railway work in all weathers, even around the glamourous Pullman trains. The hard-bitten railwayman is probably awaiting the arrival of the Bradford portion of the Up Yorkshire Pullman at 10.37am on 4th January 1961. This was the last week of the old Pullman cars for the next week they would be replaced(apart from the brake vehicles) by the new Metropolitan Cammell cars based on the BR Mk1 design. Second class car No. 74 is nearest. *Robert Anderson*

Above: Trains to London or empty coaches to Copley Hill would often be banked out of Central station by the engine which brought them in. With steam on King's Cross trains due to end the next day, A3 No. 60061 *Pretty Polly* banks the stock of its train, the 10.10am relief from King's Cross, out of the station at 2.35pm on 15th June 1963. The third coach looks interesting. The LNW/L&Y Wellington Street goods depot is on the right and "A" signal box on the left. *Robert Anderson*

Below: Recalling that long-gone Central station was where you went to catch the most glamourous expresses from Leeds, even though the terminus itself was less than celubrious. A4 Pacific No. 60006 *Sir Ralph Wedgewood* awaits departure with the White Rose to King's Cross on 16th March 1963 as a Deltic prepares to take over the northbound Queen of Scots which is standing next to it. *John Beaumont/Robert Anderson archive*

On Central's last day, guard Herbert Rowley told the Yorkshire Evening Post: "It's got a bad name with some drivers because of the falling gradient towards the buffers. But so long as you observe the 5mph approach, Central's as good as gold."

In 1960 it was claimed that Leeds train crews on the King's Cross service covered the highest daily mileage in the country.

They worked the Yorkshire Pullman to London and without barely an hour's interval returned with the 3.40pm to Leeds - a regular daily mileage of 372. Their locos were mainly A1, A3 or A4 Pacifics, some of which also worked intensively, making a round trip in 12 hours.

Wellington Street North
Booked departures & arrivals
Monday-Friday Winter 1959/60
am
12.35MX class K to Bradford
        Adolphus St.
12.45MX class K from Bradford
        Adolphus St.
3.57MX class F from King's Cross
4.47   class H from Neville Hill
5.15MO class F from Doncaster
6.40 class K from Wellington St. Sth.
8.23MX class F from Dewsnap
10.25-10.40 Neville Hill-
        Cardigan Rd. class K
10.38 class K from Wellington St Sth.
10.48 class H from Ardsley
10.50 class J from Hunslet Down
11.40 class K to Turner's Lane
pm
12.20 class K to Stourton
3.40   class K from Wellington St. Sth.
6.25   class H to Ardsley
6.45   class H to Neville Hill
6.45   class H from Turner's Lane
7.30   class K to Copley Hill LMR
8.5   class C to King's Cross
8.30   class K to Copley Hill LMR
9.22   class K to Copley Hill LMR
10.15 class K to Copley Hill LMR
10.25 class K to Bradford Valley
11.20 class J from Ardsley
Trains from Wellington St. North to the Ardsley and LNW lines had to draw out, reverse and propel from Geldard Jn. up to 'B' box, often with an assisting engine on the rear to Geldard then leading to "B" box, incoming trains undergoing the reverse procedure.

Above: The clocktower of Leeds Town Hall stands proud in this view of part of the Wellington Street North goods yard on 4th April 1970. The GN goods shed(left) is viewed from the high level(LNW/L&Y) warehouse(right) which is adjoined by the hoist used to transfer wagons between the high and low levels.
In March 1951 Wellington Street High Level was renamed Wellington Street South and Low Level Wellington Street North. On 8th June 1953 all depots were combined and re-named just Wellington Street which was probably when the wagon hoists were taken out of use. Wellington Street closed on 4th March 1974 and the site redeveloped. *Peter Rose*

Below: On 19th June 1971 an exhibition organized by the Yorkshire Post newspaper, the Blue Peter Locomotive Society and BR was held at Wellington Street. The group of youngsters under the watchful eye of the Middleton Railway Society's Derek Plummer, are keen to get one of *Great Marquess's* nameplates buffed up before the gates open. The L&Y 0-6-0 and "old gentleman's saloon" from The Railway Children movie await their public. Also on display were A2 No. 60532 *Blue Peter* and a Class 5 4-6-0. *Robert Anderson*

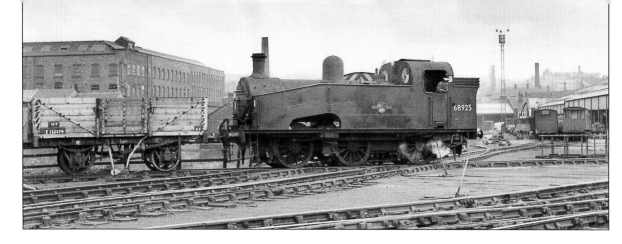

Leading north from Wellington Street low level along a narrow strip of land twixt canal and river was a fascinating backwater which survived a remarkably long time. Clinging to the core line which ended at the council highways depot on Kirkstall Road were two yards presumably named after the original owners of the land on which they stood.

Gott's Field(below left) was originally a goods depot but when photographed on 4th April 1970 was used for storing wagons and engineer's stock, especially from the Signal & Telegraph Engineer's department. *Photo by Peter Rose*

Above: With the NER goods depot in the background, J50 0-6-0T No. 68925 brings wagons from Gott's Field or beyond across to Wellington Street GN yard at 11am on 31st August 1962. *Robert Anderson*

Right: After Gott's Field the branch dived under Wellington Road to reach Montague's Field coal yard, known to local railwaymen as the "Far Yard." From here a spur swept over the canal into Greenwood & Batley's works. Both yards have since disappeared under light industrial development.

Above right: Greenwood & Batley were known for building specialist industrial locomotives, On 11th March 1977, coke car loco(works No. 420408) was under construction for British Steel Redcar coke ovens. *Adrian Booth*

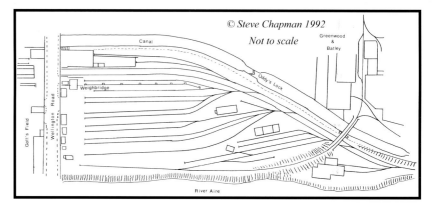

Above: At 9.28am on 15th June 1963, Copley Hill B1 No. 61214 rolls down past Armley Moor with the 9.14 Bradford Exchange to King's Cross which it will work as far as Leeds Central. Armley Moor station(Armley & Wortley until 1950) closed to passengers on 4th July 1966 but the coal depot remained in business until the 1980s. *Robert Anderson*

Below: Drafted in to cover the failures that inevitably seem to accompany the introduction of new diesels(to be fair, they were new technology then,) N7 0-6-2T No. 69694, temporarily allocated to Copley Hill but sporting a 34A King's Cross shedplate, calls at Bramley with the 3.20pm Bradford Exchange-Leeds push-pull service at 3.37 on 14th June 1954. *David Holmes*

THE WESSIE

Above: The London & North Western Railway opened the Viaduct Line in 1882 to by-pass congested Whitehall Junction and it formed the main LNW passenger route into Leeds City. York B1 No. 61031 *Reedbuck* and Class 5 4-6-0 No. 45104 storm over Water Lane, onto the viaducts and away from Leeds City with the Newcastle to Manchester Red Bank empty news vans on 29th May 1963. *Peter Rose*

Below: Ivatt Class 2 2-6-2T No. 41253 of Farnley Junction shed leaves the viaducts behind and hurries a lightweight parcels train towards Farnley Junction at 6.25pm on 12th April 1963. *Robert Anderson*

Signalling between Leeds New Station and Farnley Jn. was shown in the 1937 LMS Central Division Sectional Appendix as Absolute Block with Permissive Block on all lines between Copley Hill No.3 and Farnley Jn. for non-passenger trains. Direction of travel was Up from Leeds.

Signal boxes(with distance from previous box) were: Leeds(New) West(258yds. from Station box,) Canal Jn.(160yds.,) Viaduct (878yds.) Leeds(Wellington) Jn. (117yds. from Canal Jn.,) Whitehall Jn.(462yds.,) Whitehall Rd. (318yds.,) Copley Hill No.3 (554yds.,) Copley Hill No.2 (297yds.,), Copley Hill No.1(299yds.,) Farnley Jn. (1001yds.) Additional running lines were: Up Goods, Down Goods and Reversible Goods Copley Hill No.3-No.1.

Above: The LNW route out of Leeds - known to generations of railway staff as "The Wessie" - carries the principal TransPennine expresses. On the Viaduct line, Patriot 4-6-0 No. 45546 *Fleetwood* heads the 6.2pm Leeds-Manchester under the Leeds-Doncaster line at 6.7pm on 5th June 1960. The stretch from here to Farnley Junction was abandoned under the 1960s remodelling.

Below: Amid the changing scene near Whitehall Junction on 11th January 1967. The old Holbeck High Level station on the GN line into Central station is on the left along with severed connections to the LNW Huddersfield line. The 8F is propelling an engineers' train along the LNW line which has been relaid on a newly excavated formation to make a new junction with the GN lines at Holbeck East so that Doncaster and Bradford trains can use it to reach City station. The GN lines were slewed to join the realigned LNW line during the weekend 29th April to 1st May 1967. The two lines on the right are the original LNW lines now providing access to Whitehall Road goods yard from Whitehall Junction as wagons were by then tripped from Hunslet yard and not Copley Hill. The Monk Bridge iron works stands beyond the various goods wagons. *Both Robert Anderson*

Above: Between Whitehall Junction and Farnley Junction were the extensive former LNW Copley Hill sidings which were both goods sorting sidings and carriage sidings. At 3.52pm on Saturday 2nd March 1963 "Black Five" No. 45079 on the right has just uncoupled from an incoming freight - possibly the 3.15pm Saturdays Only from Wellington Street North - as sister loco 45080 departs with the 3.55 to Huddersfield Hillhouse. Copley Hill No.2 Shunting signal box is in the middle of it all. A turntable, cattle dock and carriage sheds were situated immediately behind the photographer. Nowadays, only the two main running lines beyond the carriages on the left remain but the site of the sidings can still be discerned from passing TransPennine trains. *Robert Anderson*

Copley Hill. Gravitating trains from No.1 to No.3 box: On arrival of Down trains at No.1 box the signalman will instruct the driver if his train is to be gravitated. Trains must not be gravitated from No.1 to No.3 box unless there is a train, engine, brake van, or not less than three wagons properly secured, standing at No.3 Down Main home signal. The fireman will, in the case of a train which has to be gravitated, detach the engine which will run ahead into No.1 Up and Down Loop or No.2 Up Loop. Guards must, after putting on the brake to hold the train, ascertain from the signalman if the train is to be gravitated towards No.3 box, and on the inner home signal for Copley Hill No.1 being lowered gravitate the wagons down to the train, engine, brake van or wagons in front, to which he must attach his train....*1937 LMS Central Division Sectional Appendix*

Below: On Sunday 27th August 1961 rebuilt Patriot 4-6-0 No. 45545 *Planet* of Crewe North shed passes the remains of Farnley & Wortley station on its way into Leeds along the Viaduct Line. This station replaced the original(beyond the loco on the right) when the Viaduct Line was built but was itself closed on 3rd November 1952. *Peter Rose*

Above: Farnley Junction looking west on 17th September 1961 as a pair of 4-6-0s pass with the Newcastle to Manchester Red Bank empty news vans. On the extreme left is the start of the flying junction leading to the New Line, while the engine sheds are in the middle and the hostel used by locomotive crews on lodging turns is on the right. The Leeds-bound track of the New Line flying junction is immediately to the left of the signal while the Farnley branch goes off to the right. *Peter Rose*

Farnley Junction replaced an earlier 3-road shed adjoining the LNWR's 4-road carriage shed at the Farnley end of Copley Hill sidings, the first then becoming another carriage shed. It was coded 25G under the London Midland Region Wakefield district but on transfer to the NE Region in 1956 it became 55C in the Leeds district. It was a mixed traffic depot providing everything from goods and shunting engines to express passenger engines for the Trans-Pennine route out of Leeds; on summer Saturdays its passenger engines ventured to the Yorkshire coast. The depot was situated in the triangle formed by the main lines, the Farnley branch and a west-south spur between the two which actually formed part of the depot, the mechanical coaling plant being situated on a loop parallel to the spur. It consisted of a 12-road straight shed complete with adjacent water tank covering two more tracks, and outdoor lifting gear. There was no turntable, engines being turned on the triangle.

ALLOCATED TO FARNLEY JUNCTION NOVEMBER 1966

LOCOMOTIVES ALLOCATED TO FARNLEY JUNCTION JANUARY 1957

2P 4-4-0: 40581/84; Ivatt Class 2 2-6-2T 41254-59; 6P5F "Crab" 2-6-0: 42702/13/66/89/865/66; Class 5 4-6-0: 44896/5063/75/79/80/5204/11; Jubilee 4-6-0: 45581 *Bihar & Orissa*/45646 *Napier*/45695 *Minotaur*/45708 *Resolution;* 3F 0-6-0T: 47567-71; WD 2-8-0: 90127/254/308/18/22/336/51/95/407/562/88/91/645/9/50/64/66/84/98/99/711/26/28. Total: 53

Class 5 4-6-0: 44826/96/943; Jubilee 4-6-0: 45562 *Alberta*/ 45647 *Sturdee*; 8F 2-8-0: 48080/ 664; 350hp 0-6-0: D3652/3/6/8. Total: 11

Right: Stanier Class 5 4-6-0 No. 45080 poses outside the shed on 6th August 1966.
The building on the right is the matron's house for the locomen's hostel.
Adrian Booth

Above: Inside Farnley Junction shed on 1st August 1965. Class 5 No. 44826 heads the line with 44765(fitted with Timken roller bearings and a double chimney,) and "Crab" 2-6-0 42942 behind it. Jubilee 45581 *Bihar and Orissa* is on the right. *Peter Rose*

Centre: Two of Farnley's Jubilees on parade outside the shed on 19th November 1966, just four days before the shed closed. Both Nos. 45562 *Alberta* (nearest) and 45647 *Sturdee*(cleanest) were transferred to Holbeck. *Sturdee* was withdrawn in April 1967 but *Alberta* went on to become the last Jubilee in service, not being withdrawn until November 1967. *Adrian Booth*

Bottom: The back of Farnley Junction shed where withdrawn "Crab" 2-6-0s, 42766 the nearest, line the spur by-passing the coaling plant on the left. On the right, an 8F 2-8-0 stands at the ash disposal plant. *John Beaumont*

Above: Class 3F 0-6-0T No. 47420 shunts a load of steel over the A58 road bridge on the Farnley branch on 14th January 1961. The branch served Farnley iron works(ahead of 47420) which later became the fireclay works. Latterly, it served Dunlop & Ranken's steel mill and stockholders to the right. It survived in use until the late 1980s. Right: This NER-style slotted signal once protected the entrance to the works. *Both Peter Rose*

The Eastern Region Sectional Appendix 1969 stated that the Farnley branch was single track and 1 mile 200yds long. The maximum speed was 25mph in both directions. It gave the following instructions: "The signals controlling movements to and from the branch are electrically controlled to prevent more than one train or engine being on the branch at the same time. The branch is worked under regulations for working single lines by One Engine in Steam....but no train staff is provided.

"Keys for the padlock securing the ground frame at the Farnley Branch Junction end of Dunlop & Ranken's sidings are kept at....the depots of guards working over this branch...."

The 1937 LMS Sectional Appendix stated that the branch was worked "One Engine in Steam or two or more engines coupled together" with a square, red staff handed to drivers by the Farnley Junction signalman. It also stated that "to a point where lines converge near Whitehall Road bridge" it was Up and Down lines with no block signalling and that fixed signals were in use.

Below: In torrential rain on 1st August 1966 Jubilee No. 45647 *Sturdee* thrashes the 09.50 Leeds-Blackpool excursion past its home depot where visiting Standard Class 5 No. 73011 prepares to work the 10.22 Leeds City-Belle Vue excursion. *Robert Anderson*

Above: "Black Fives" 44911 and 44943 pass the new rail-connected Cadbury's distribution depot as they storm away from Farnley Junction on the Dewsbury line with the Newcastle-Manchester Red Bank vans on Sunday 2nd June 1963. Farnley provided power for this train on Sundays. The Up road of the New Line to Huddersfield passes behind Cadbury's depot. *Peter Rose*

Below: Without doubt Farnley's most prolific engine was Jubilee No. 45581 *Bihar & Orissa* which always seemed to put on a show. Here, with her usual zeal, she restarts from a signal check just after Farnley Junction with the empty stock for excursion 1X86 - possibly a Morley Low to Blackpool excursion - at 9.14am on 16th June 1962. She was withdrawn in August 1966. The Down road of the New Line comes in from the left. *Robert Anderson*